Drums and Guns

Revolution in Ulster

Drums and Guns

Revolution in Ulster

MARTIN WALLACE

 GEOFFREY CHAPMAN
LONDON DUBLIN MELBOURNE 1970

Geoffrey Chapman Ltd
18 High Street, Wimbledon, London SW19

Geoffrey Chapman (Ireland) Ltd
5–7 Main Street, Blackrock, County Dublin

Geoffrey Chapman Pty Ltd
346 St Kilda Road, Melbourne, Vic 3004, Australia

First published 1970

SBN 225 48927 9

This book is set in 11 *pt Baskerville (2 point leaded)*
Made and printed in Great Britain by Butler & Tanner Ltd, Frome and London

Contents

To My Wife

Preface

Most of this book is concerned with very recent events—
Captain Terence O'Neill's attempts to heal some of Ulster's
persistent divisions, the civil rights campaign, the violence of
August 1969 and its aftermath. As a journalist, I have in
different ways been involved in much of what is described in
this book, but I have not hesitated to draw on the work of
many professional colleagues. I would like to acknowledge my
debt to them, and at the same time record my admiration for
their unfailing courage in reporting Ulster's troubles.

The sections of the book which delve further into history are
necessarily less detailed. I have not attempted a comprehensive
history of Ulster, but have concentrated on elements which seem
to have special relevance to recent events. Andrew Boyd's
recent book, *Holy War in Belfast* (1969), was particularly valuable
for its accounts of earlier rioting in Belfast. J. C. Beckett's
The Making of Modern Ireland, 1603–1923 (1966) is an outstanding academic work, but well worth reading are *The Course of
Irish History*, edited by T. W. Moody and F. X. Martin (1967),
and *Two Centuries of Irish History*, edited by James Hawthorne
(1966). The events in Ulster which led to the partition of
Ireland are well described in A. T. Q. Stewart's *The Ulster
Crisis* (1967) and Hugh Shearman's *Not an Inch* (1942). There
are useful chapters in *The Years of the Great Test, 1926–39*,
edited by Francis MacManus (1967), and *Belfast: Origin and
Growth of an Industrial City*, edited by J. C. Beckett and R. E.
Glasscock (1967).

On the constitutional side, Nicholas Mansergh's *The
Government of Northern Ireland: A Study in Devolution* (1936)

remains a most illuminating work. Parts of *Ulster Under Home Rule: A Study of the Political and Economic Problems of Northern Ireland*, edited by Thomas Wilson (1955), are also relevant. More recently, Harry Calvert's *Constitutional Law in Northern Ireland: A Study in Regional Government* (1968) probes many of the questions posed by Stormont's existence as a subordinate parliament.

The report of the Cameron commission, *Disturbances in Northern Ireland* (Cmd. 532, 1969), the accompanying *Commentary* indicating the Northern Ireland Government's reform programme (Cmd. 534), and the Hunt committee's report, *Police in Northern Ireland* (Cmd. 535, 1969), are all important and informative documents. In *Burntollet* (1969), Bowes Egan and Vincent McCormack have reconstructed the course of a civil rights march which was critical to the development of events in Northern Ireland. A collection of O'Neill's speeches has been published under the title *Ulster at the Crossroads* (1969).

Finally, the most valuable study of Protestant–Catholic relations is *The Northern Ireland Problem: A Study in Group Relations* by Denis P. Barritt and Charles F. Carter (1962). Innumerable Protestants and Catholics have also helped to form my views on the nature of Ulster's divisions, not least my fellow members of the Irish Association for Cultural, Economic and Social Relations.

Belfast
January 1970

1. Bloody August

It began on 12 August 1969, in Londonderry. This was the day of the annual Apprentice Boys' march, celebrating the 15-week siege of the city in 1689, when Protestants held out against James II's army. The original thirteen apprentice boys had shut the city's gates against troops sent to garrison Derry in James's interest.

From mid-morning, Apprentice Boys—old men as well as young—had gathered from all over Northern Ireland, taking possession of Derry's ancient walls and demonstrating to the Roman Catholic majority in the city that the Protestant ascendancy was not yet ended. The bands played Orange tunes, the streets were decked with red-white-and-blue bunting, and the marchers largely conducted themselves with Protestant sobriety. Occasionally, the bands played a little louder as they passed Catholic bystanders, and sometimes a coin was tossed contemptuously down from the high walls to the narrow streets and hovels of the Catholic Bogside area. Many people had urged that the Northern Ireland Government summon up its courage and ban a Protestant parade, and many others had said the parade should go ahead and test Derry's willingness to live in peace with itself and tolerate different politico-religious views. The Apprentice Boys knew the world was watching and expecting trouble.

It came in mid-afternoon. The Apprentice Boys had left the walled city, marching down Shipquay Street from the central Diamond, through one of the massive arches which breach the walls, and out along the Strand Road, returning by a slightly different and safer route. The trouble began in Waterloo

Place, beneath one corner of the walls and at the point where Waterloo Street and William Street lead into the Bogside.

As the afternoon wore on, a small group of Catholic youths stood behind crush barriers and jeered at the marchers. The Apprentice Boys marched impassively on, even as the youths joined derisively in the Orange songs the bands were playing. Then the first stones were thrown from William Street and Waterloo Street. Bottles and bricks followed, and even marbles were catapulted at the parade and its supporters beyond. The Apprentice Boys protected themselves as best they could and marched on, while some of their supporters returned the Catholics' fire. The police put on their riot equipment, helmets and shields, and drew their batons.

Stewards of Derry's civil rights movement tried to push the Catholic youths back. John Hume, the young civil rights leader who had become an Independent M.P. in the Northern Ireland general election the previous February, appealed for peace. So did Eddie McAteer, the leader of the Nationalist Party, whom he had unseated. As the parade passed, the situation became the familiar Derry confrontation between police and Bogsiders. Stone-throwing broke out where other streets led out of the Bogside. Some of the Catholic youths wore nylon masks to prevent identification.

Barricades were hastily erected in Bogside. They consisted of scaffolding, barbed wire, bricks, paving stones, traffic signs, planks—anything that would keep the police and Protestants out. Ultimately they worked, but first the police— who had been stoned continuously—made a series of baton charges. Rattling their batons against their riot shields, they cleared Waterloo Street, in the shadow of the city walls. Armoured cars and water cannon moved into William Street. One armoured car was set on fire by a petrol bomb. At one point, Protestants stormed along behind the police, joining in the assault on the Bogsiders with bricks and lead piping, then dropping behind to stone the windows of Catholic houses in Rossville Street.

But the Bogsiders had been prepared for trouble. A high

block of flats towering above the mean streets provided an impregnable vantage point. From the roof, a small group of youths and girls tossed petrol bombs every time the police gained an advantage below. Above them flew the green-white-and-orange tricolour of the Republic of Ireland. Young children brought up cardboard boxes filled with petrol bombs produced by the women of Bogside.

In a terrace house deep in Bogside, the committee of the Derry Citizens' Defence Association implemented its plans for a new siege. The association had been formed after riots in July, following the annual Orange celebrations, and its stewards had tried in vain to prevent trouble during the Apprentice Boys' march. Its chairman was a veteran Irish Republican, Sean Keenan, but many shades of political opinion were represented. The committee's plans included first aid posts, fire-fighting, prevention of looting, and a network of short-wave radios which allowed the Bogsiders to anticipate police moves.

The battle still raged as darkness fell and the night sky was lit by flames from a huge fire in a William Street bakery. A warehouse and a petrol station were alight, and families were evacuated from burning houses. Many of the barricades were set alight. A number of shots were fired during the night, and a breadserver was wounded in the shoulder.

Earlier in the evening, Tom Caldwell, an Independent Unionist M.P. from Belfast who had backed former Premier Terence O'Neill at the general election, telephoned Northern Ireland's Minister of Home Affairs, Robert Porter, from Derry to urge the use of tear gas. At midnight, the first volley of CS tearsmoke canisters landed among the Bogsiders behind the burning barricade in William Street. With tears streaming down their cheeks, the choking rioters fell back. Many of them lay vomiting on the streets. But sporadic fighting continued through the night, and by morning 94 policeman had been injured and 13 were still in hospital. The official figures for civilians were lower, but took no account of the medical treatment given within what one Bogsider called Hell's Half Acre.

During the night, an ominous warning came from the Northern Ireland Civil Rights Association. It said:

> A war of genocide is about to flare across the North. The C.R.A. demands that all Irishmen recognise their common interdependence and calls upon the Government and people of the Twenty-Six Counties to act now to prevent a great national disaster. We urgently request that the Government take immediate action to have a United Nations peace-keeping force sent to Derry, and if necessary Ireland should recall her peace-keeping troops from Cyprus for service at home. Pending the arrival of a United Nations force we urge immediate suspension of the Six-County Government and the partisan R.U.C. and B Specials and their temporary replacement by joint peace-keeping patrols of Irish and British forces. We urge immediate consultation between the Irish and British Governments to this end. Time has run out in the North.

Behind the barricades, a statement came from Bernadette Devlin, the 22-year-old student who had taken the Mid-Ulster seat at Westminster from the Unionists in a May by-election, and civil rights leader Eamonn McCann. It said: "The barricades in the Bogside of Derry must not be taken down until the Westminster Government states its clear commitment to the suspension of the constitution of Northern Ireland and calls immediately a constitutional conference representative of Westminster, the Unionist Government, the Government of the Republic of Ireland and all tendencies within the civil rights movement."

Meanwhile, the Northern Ireland Cabinet Security Committee had been meeting the heads of the Royal Ulster Constabulary at police headquarters in Belfast. Early in the morning, the Minister of Home Affairs made an order under the 1951 Public Order Act to prohibit all public processions and outdoor meetings for the rest of August. The ban, which was later extended, would first affect the Ancient Order of Hibernians' annual celebrations on 15 August, then the traditional parades of the Protestant Black Institution at the end of the month. Only the Salvation Army was exempted.

The fighting in Derry continued sporadically throughout Wednesday, 13 August, and police continued to use tearsmoke. But a message had gone out from Sean Keenan to Frank Gogarty, a Belfast dentist who was chairman of the Civil Rights Association, asking him to organise meetings in various parts of Northern Ireland in an attempt to divert police from Bogside. The previous night, police stations in Coalisland, Strabane and Newry had been attacked by hostile crowds. On Wednesday night, violence spread to towns like Lurgan, Enniskillen and Armagh. In Belfast, police stations at Andersonstown, Springfield Road and Hastings Street—all Catholic areas—were attacked. If the demonstrations were intended to be non-violent diversionary exercises, they quickly got out of hand.

In Dungannon, fires were started at the courthouse, the labour exchange and a newspaper office. In Dungiven, an Orange hall was burned down. In Enniskillen, police were attacked at a Catholic housing estate as they tried to break up a meeting held in defiance of the Government's ban. In Newry, lorries were commandeered to block main routes. In Lurgan, rival Protestant and Catholic crowds threw stones and bottles. In most of the trouble spots, police were on the defensive and often penned in by petrol bomb attacks and fusillades of stones and bottles. Occasionally, they were able to make baton charges.

Derry was still in flames. A large shirt factory in William Street blazed spectacularly, and tyres burned in a nearby depot. A disused bakery was gutted. Policemen fired shots in the air when they were hard pressed by a barrage of petrol bombs. During the night, the Bogsiders regained ground they had previously lost to the police. There were running battles between Protestants and Catholics for most of the night. The police continued to use CS tearsmoke, but the Bogsiders began to get used to it. They uncovered a supply of war-time gas masks, and found that the hot air from burning tyres helped to lift the gas into the air. Through the night, a number of shots were fired, and Protestant mobs roamed through other parts of the city. At one point the City Hotel, where many visiting journalists were staying, was under siege and some cars were thrown into the nearby River Foyle.

But, throughout the months of sporadic disturbances in Northern Ireland, the great fear had always been that serious trouble would spread to Belfast. Wednesday night was the beginning, and barricades started to go up in the Catholic Falls Road area in West Belfast, sealing it off from police who had withdrawn after several baton charges. The barricades were largely built of material which had been collected for the traditional 15 August bonfires, and they were quickly set alight. One barricade set fire to a mill in Northumberland Street. A car showroom was set on fire, and cars pulled out for use in the barricades. In the Crumlin Road area, where Protestant and Catholic streets abut, hostile crowds threw petrol bombs. Shots were fired in several streets.

Early on Wednesday evening, Major James Chichester-Clark, the Prime Minister of Northern Ireland, broadcast an appeal for peace. "There is absolutely no legitimate political reason for tearing apart this community of ours," he said. "Violence will not enact one moment sooner those reforming measures which are already proceeding with all possible speed—reform of the local government franchise, machinery to deal with citizens' grievances, the establishment of an impartial commission to draw electoral boundaries and so on. ... The more basic problems of housing and unemployment can be cured only by effort and time." He promised that if the rioters of Bogside withdrew peacefully to their homes and observed the law, no retribution would fall on them. Major Chichester-Clark also announced the recall of the Northern Ireland Parliament, and said that the Ulster Special Constabulary—an auxiliary force, wholly Protestant and known as the B Specials—would be used to the full, not for riot or crowd control, but to relieve the regular police of other duties.

But a more momentous broadcast was made in Dublin the

same evening. The Prime Minister of the Republic of Ireland, Jack Lynch, announced in an emotional voice that the Irish Government had requested the British Government to apply immediately to the United Nations for the urgent despatch of a peace-keeping force to Northern Ireland. He added: "Recognising, however, that the reunification of the national territory can provide the only permanent solution for the problem, it is our intention to request the British Government to enter into early negotiations with the Irish Government to review the present constitutional position of the six counties of Northern Ireland." Lynch said the British Government had been asked to see that police attacks on the people of Derry should cease immediately. He said that many of the injured did not wish to be treated in Northern Ireland hospitals, and that the Irish Army had been directed to set up field hospitals in County Donegal adjacent to Derry and at other points along the border where they might be necessary. Prime Minister Lynch said it was evident that the Northern Ireland Government was no longer in control of a situation which was the inevitable outcome of the policies pursued for decades by successive Stormont governments. "It is obvious that the R.U.C. is no longer accepted as an impartial police force," he said. "Neither would the employment of British troops be acceptable, nor would they be likely to restore peace conditions —certainly not in the long term."

Was partition to become a live issue in Irish politics again? Chichester-Clark replied immediately: "This clumsy and intolerable intrusion into our internal affairs will be deeply resented by the majority of people in Northern Ireland. His idea that Northern Ireland is to be bartered for in spite of the repeated affirmations of the will of its own electorate dies hard. . . . I must hold Mr Lynch personally responsible for any worsening of feeling which these inflammatory and ill-considered remarks may cause." The Northern Premier's terse rebuke was echoed in more diplomatic language by the Foreign and Commonwealth Office in London. A statement said the British Government "have no intention of departing from pledges previously given that Northern Ireland should not cease to be a part of the United Kingdom without the consent of the people of Northern Ireland".

The battles continued in the streets, and on Thursday the hard-pressed regular police in Derry were joined by B Specials, despite the assurance given by Chichester-Clark the previous evening. The deployment of B Specials on riot duty was short-lived, but in Belfast it would contribute significantly to the deterioration of the situation. Parliament reassembled at Stormont in the afternoon, and Chichester-Clark formally brought to an end the period of improved North–South relations inaugurated by the 1965 meeting of O'Neill and Lynch's predecessor, Sean Lemass. "History will record in how responsible and neighbourly a way we have tried to conduct our relationships with the Irish Republic. All that has been brought to an end by this intervention. We must and we will treat the Government which seeks to wound us in our darkest hour as an unfriendly and implacable Government, dedicated to overthrow by any means the status which enjoys the support of a majority of our electorate."

The Prime Minister defended the decision not to ban the Apprentice Boys' parade. "There was no evidence whatever that those in the parade intended to act in any way irresponsibly. Nor was there any evidence of an organised plan to interfere with them. . . . We also had to take into account that if a disciplined and orderly parade was banned, a right to parade on that day exercised over countless years might be asserted by other and less well-disciplined elements."

From the Opposition benches, Gerry Fitt, the Republican Labour M.P. who represented the Dock constituency at Stormont and West Belfast at Westminster, said the Government no longer had any relevance in the affairs of the Irish people. All but one of the Opposition M.P.s walked out of the House. But the most dramatic moment came when the Minister of Home Affairs, Robert Porter, rose to announce quietly: "The Inspector-General of the R.U.C. has made a request to the G.O.C. Northern Ireland for the deployment of troops in Londonderry in aid of the civil power. The G.O.C. has acceded to this request. This step has been taken with the knowledge and full approval of the United Kingdom and Northern Ireland Governments."

The troops—300 men of the Prince of Wales' Own Regiment, with steel helmets, automatic rifles and Stirling sub-machine guns—moved out of H.M.S. *Sea Eagle*, the naval base across the River Foyle, late on Thursday afternoon. Within minutes of crossing Craigavon Bridge, peace had been restored. The Bogsiders were celebrating victory over the police and B Specials, and the troops were cordoning off the Bogside with barbed-wire entanglements. Later in the evening, the Derry Citizens' Defence Association Committee announced the terms of a cease-fire agreed with the officer commanding the troops in Derry. It included the withdrawal of B Specials from the Derry area. The barricades remained, though the troops were given cups of tea by the Bogsiders and treated like an army of liberation. The police stayed out of sight.

In London, the British Home Secretary, James Callaghan, said: "The G.O.C. Northern Ireland has been instructed to take all the necessary steps, acting impartially between citizen and citizen, to restore law and order. Troops will be withdrawn as soon as this is accomplished. This is a limited operation, and during it the troops will remain in direct and exclusive control of the G.O.C., who will continue to be responsible to the United Kingdom Government." The Home Secretary's statement went on: "The Ireland Act of 1949 affirms that neither Northern Ireland nor any part of it will in any event cease to be part of the United Kingdom without the consent of the Parliament of Northern Ireland, and the United Kingdom Government reaffirms the pledges previously given that this will remain the position so long as the people of Northern Ireland wish."

There were no troops in Belfast, and four people were shot dead during the night. The whole truth will never be known, but one factor was certainly the decision to mobilise the B Specials and deploy them in the tangle of streets separating the

Catholic Falls Road and the Protestant Shankill Road. The Catholic reaction was to throw up defensive barricades constructed of sawn-down telegraph poles, old furniture, paving stones, anything that burned. Not long after the public houses closed at ten o'clock, the fighting began. Police armoured cars drove into the barricades, and were met with petrol bombs. Protestant crowds, spoiling for a fight, massed behind the police and B Specials. Petrol bombs and bricks flew across the ill-defined, changing no-man's land which separated Protestant and Catholic mobs.

Well before midnight, firing began. A police statement said later: "It is of paramount importance that the public should know that the police did not open fire in Belfast last night until they themselves had come under heavy gunfire almost simultaneously in various parts of the city. Automatic weapons were used in these attacks against the police. The force fired purely in self-defence." Whatever the truth of this, the morning brought evidence that rows of Catholic houses and flats had been raked with bullets from automatic weapons. In Divis Towers, a high block of flats, one of many bullets killed nine-year-old Patrick Rooney. His father, shipyard worker Cornelius Rooney, had moved his family into a back room for safety.

Trooper Hugh McCabe, on leave from Germany, was also shot dead in Divis Towers. Mrs Marie Skinner later said he died pushing her and another woman down as police fired into the flats. "The armoured car came flying down Divis Street from the direction of the barracks. He was taking pot luck. He was firing at anything he could see." She said Trooper McCabe had been making petrol bombs—their only means of defence.

Whole streets were burned into rubble. In the Catholic residents' version, Protestant mobs followed B Specials, whose firing forced the Catholics out. Then each house in turn was set alight. Anything that survived the fire was smashed. Gas meters were broken open for the money in them. The worst of the fighting was concentrated in a comparatively thin wedge of streets along the lower Falls Road and its continuation in Divis Street, where the adjoining police station in Hastings Street was under attack for the second night running. Herbert Roy, a Protestant, was shot in Dover Street, where some of the fiercest fighting occurred. But there was trouble in a wide area of West Belfast, and many Catholic-owned public houses and bookmakers' offices were burned and looted. On the other side of the Shankill Road is the Crumlin Road, along which there had been earlier clashes between Catholics and Protestants or police. Here, Samuel McLarnon was shot dead in his house in Herbert Street. Eye-witnesses said a hail of bullets came from an armoured vehicle as he sat in his kitchen.

There were disturbances in other parts of Northern Ireland. In Armagh, 31-year-old John Gallagher was shot dead in Cathedral Road when a volley of shots was fired into a crowd of civil rights demonstrators. Another man was taken to hospital with leg wounds. A police statement issued the following day said that no police personnel had been on duty in Cathedral Road at the time of the shooting. This was untrue, and the local county inspector subsequently told a coroner's court that a decision not to correct the statement had been made by "higher authorities". That night, 17 B Specials from nearby Tynan had been in Armagh police station, and had been instructed to get into their cars and follow the county inspector; during the journey, he lost sight of them. Witnesses at the inquest described how shots were fired by men in dark uniforms, but none of the Specials was prepared to give evidence, although in statements some had admitted firing into the air. "One thing is definite," said the coroner, "that the firing which killed John Gallagher was not lawful firing."

Friday brought the first breach in the ban on public processions, when more than 1,000 members of the Ancient Order of Hibernians paraded through Dungiven. When two police officers warned the organisers that they would be breaking the law, the reply was: "Dungiven is 90 per cent Catholic. If Orange riff-raff can march through it, why can't we?" Riot police had moved into the local barracks, but made no attempt to halt the parade. The crowd which followed the marchers cheered loudest as it passed the burnt-out Orange hall.

In Belfast, sporadic sniping continued throughout the day, and smoke from many fires rose above the city. The largest fire was at a mill at the foot of Falls Road, believed to have been used by roof-top snipers. For hour after hour, Catholic families from the warren of tiny streets separating the Falls and Shankill Roads left their homes in search of safety. They carried bundles of clothing and food under their arms, and furniture was taken in lorries. Schools and church halls became refuge centres, as Catholics moved deeper into their traditional ghettoes. Some refugees loaded their possessions into cars and drove to relatives outside the city. Many crossed the border into the Republic of Ireland, and there were long queues at Great Victoria Street station for trains to Dublin. Men who had stayed away from work spent the day barricading houses, shops and public houses. Corporation buses were commandeered to make barricades, and burned through the day. The rubble of destroyed houses was piled together to protect the homes that remained.

The death-roll rose to six, when 15-year-old Gerald McAuley was shot during the afternoon in Kashmir Road, close to Clonard Monastery, which had been continuously under fire from snipers. Michael Lynch, wounded during the previous night's gun battles, died in hospital. As 600 men of the 3rd battalion, the Light Infantry, flew into Northern Ireland, Prime Minister Chichester-Clark telephoned the Home Secretary, and it was agreed to move troops into Belfast. In the Republic, first-line troops were also mobilised "so as to ensure they will be in readiness for participation in peace-keeping operations".

Chichester-Clark, speaking on the steps of Stormont Castle, said it was clear that subversive Republican elements were to the fore in the events of the previous evening, and that there had been an evident plan to attack the police. "I am in no doubt that Ulster faces today the most serious and malevolent threat in its history. . . . The United Kingdom and Northern Ireland Governments stand together in their complete determination that we will not be forced out of the United Kingdom against our will." He announced that a number of persons suspected of subversive activities were being held by the police for interrogation. That evening, two senior police officers from Britain—Robert Mark, Deputy Commissioner of the London Metropolitan Police, and Douglas Osmond, Chief Constable of Hampshire—arrived for "liaison and consultation".

The troops—men of the Royal Regiment of Wales and the Queen's Regiment—moved into the Falls Road–Divis Street area with fixed bayonets to man barbed-wire barricades separating the main Protestant and Catholic areas. At one point, tear gas was used against a crowd which tried to storm a barricade, but generally the arrival of soldiers brought a lowering of tension. But there were still no troops in the Ardoyne district, at the top of the Crumlin Road, and Catholics there complained that B Specials had fired indiscriminately from an armoured car in Hooker Street and Butler Street. It was in this area that 48-year-old David Linton was shot to death. Police put the casualty figures in the 24 hours to 7.0 a.m. on Saturday at more than 300, with 74 detained in hospital. The previous night's figures had been 127 treated in hospital, 67 detained.

The weekend was comparatively quiet, although sniping continued in Belfast on Saturday. Fires continued to burn, and firemen were often held back by barricades or by shots. During the day, troops took up position in the Crumlin Road area. It emerged that 24 men were being held for interrogation under the Special Powers Act; the Act allowed them to be held without charge for 48 hours, and the Minister of Home Affairs later made orders under the Act by which they could be held for a further seven days. Church leaders appealed for peace, and there began to emerge in different parts of the city joint Protestant–Catholic peace committees whose vigilantes patrolled at night. On Sunday night, a police station in Crossmaglen, Co. Armagh, was attacked by armed men who drove a lorry containing a land-mine up to the guardroom; a grenade failed to explode the land-mine, and the attackers fled under fire.

At Stormont Castle, on Sunday, 17 August, Major Chichester-Clark gave a Press conference in which he defended the decision to permit the Apprentice Boys' march five days before. "The fact of the matter," he said, "is that although various people expressed some anxiety about the proposed march, absolutely no evidence came to hand of plans either to behave violently on the march or to mount violent opposition to it. . . . The clear message coming to us out of Londonderry was that every responsible element in the city wanted to achieve a day free from any sort of disorder." He denied, quite rightly, that there had been any slowing down or reversal of the Government's reform programme and added: "The real cause of the disorder is to be found in the activities of extreme Republican elements and others determined to overthrow our state. That is why we have found it necessary to detain a considerable number of known and dangerous agitators." The Prime Minister recalled that the chief of staff of the Irish Republican Army, Cathal Goulding, had said that his organisation had given leadership, helping with "stones, petrol bombs and other traditional methods of defence".

Chichester-Clark repeated his criticism of the Dublin Government. All it had done was "to convince us for all time that we must look elsewhere for our friends. We held out our hand to them as good neighbours. They have behaved much like those hooligans who have used the present troubles as an excuse to burn their neighbours out." He defended the use of B Specials in the context of mounting disorder. "How could we have faced our consciences had we allowed such a situation to persist without calling in rapidly such reserves as were available to us?"

It was, from the Government's viewpoint, a disastrous Press conference, for journalists from all over the world immediately began to pick holes in the Prime Minister's statement. They had certainly warned of trouble in Londonderry; if the Government was so ill-informed a few days ago, how was it suddenly so well informed on the causes of disorder? Why were most of the dead Catholics, and why were most of homes destroyed

in Catholic areas? Chichester-Clark admitted under questioning that the B Specials were not a completely trained and
disciplined force. When reporters told of seeing B Specials
mixing with armed Protestants, the Minister of Home Affairs,
Robert Porter, said they should report misconduct. To whom?
To the police. The Press conference dissolved in derisive
laughter.

This was perhaps the last time that the Government took so
simple a view of a complex situation. On Tuesday, there was
to be a visit to Downing Street. On Monday evening, when
Chichester-Clark called a peace conference of Protestant and
Catholic moderates at Stormont Castle, he heard some very
plain speaking from men who in some quarters would be
labelled "tame Catholics". On Monday, there also came a
warning from the G.O.C., Lieutenant-General Sir Ian Freeland, that the Army's honeymoon period might soon come to
an end unless something constructive and helpful emerged from
Downing Street.

Belfast settled into an uneasy peace. Many public houses,
owned by Catholics, had been wrecked in different parts of
the city. Others closed early, as did licensed clubs. Cinemas
cut out their evening performances, and bus services were
restricted. Behind the Catholic barricades, local defence committees imposed a 9.0 p.m. curfew. Elsewhere, there were
reports of continued intimidation, and Catholic families continued to move out of "mixed" areas under threat of violence.
A smaller number of Protestant families also left their homes.
The first of the pirate radios, Radio Free Belfast, had begun
to broadcast from behind the barricades. Radio Free Derry
was also broadcasting behind the barricades of Bogside.

In Dublin, a statement from the I.R.A. said that Northern
units "have been in action in defence of the lives and homes
of the people which have been attacked by deliberately
fomented sectarian forces backed by the Specials with the aim
of destroying the natural solidarity and unity of working class
people. . . . The people of the Falls Road have grateful acknow-
ledged this assistance in the past few days and have contrasted

it bitterly with the failure of the Dublin Government to act in their defence." The Dublin Government was active, however, in bringing the Northern Ireland situation to the attention of the United Nations. The Minister for External Affairs, Dr Patrick Hillery—who on Friday had described an unsatisfactory meeting with Lord Chalfont, Minister of State at the Foreign and Commonwealth Office, as a "brush-off"—was already in New York lobbying members of the Security Council.

The Downing Street talks on Tuesday, 19 August, lasted five hours. Chichester-Clark was accompanied by the Deputy Premier, Senator John Andrews (son of Northern Ireland's second Prime Minister), the Minister of Development, Brian Faulkner, and Home Minister Porter. With Prime Minister Harold Wilson were Home Secretary Callaghan, Foreign Secretary Michael Stewart, Defence Minister Denis Healey, and Lord Stonham, Joint Minister of State at the Home Office. Earlier Wilson, who had broken his holiday in the Scillies because of the Ulster crisis, had held a full meeting of the British Cabinet. At one point in the Downing Street talks, the two parties broke for separate discussions.

At the end, there was both a communiqué and a seven-point declaration setting out the future course of relations between Whitehall and Stormont. The declaration reaffirmed earlier pledges about Northern Ireland's position within the United Kingdom, and said: "The border is not an issue." It affirmed that responsibility for affairs in Northern Ireland was entirely a matter of domestic jurisdiction—in other words, not a matter for the Republic of Ireland or the United Nations. It asserted the United Kingdom Government's ultimate responsibility for the protection of people living in Northern Ireland, but said that troops would be withdrawn when law and order had been restored. Both Governments reaffirmed that "in all legislation and executive decisions of Government, every citizen of Northern Ireland is entitled to the same equality of treatment and freedom from discrimination as obtains in the rest of the United Kingdom, irrespective of political views or religion".

The most significant sentence said: "In the context of the commitment of these troops, the Northern Ireland Government have reaffirmed their intention to take into the fullest account at all times the views of Her Majesty's Government in the United Kingdom, especially in relation to matters affecting the status of citizens of that part of the United Kingdom and their equal rights and protection under the law." The communiqué indicated the extent of the British Government's new involvement in Northern Ireland's affairs. Two senior civil servants were to be stationed in Belfast; it later emerged that one would be in the Cabinet offices, the other in the Ministry of Home Affairs. The G.O.C. Northern Ireland was to assume overall responsibility for security operations, including full command of the B Specials, who would be rapidly relieved of riot and crowd control duties. The two Governments would discuss as a matter of urgency the future of the civilian security services; soon afterwards, Lord Hunt was named as head of an advisory body, along with Robert Mark and Sir James Robertson, Chief Constable of Glasgow. There was also to be an impartial investigation into recent disorders. An appeal was to be made for unauthorised arms to be handed in under an amnesty. The question of detainees was discussed.

As the talks were coming to an end, Wilson appeared on television. He made it clear that direct rule from Westminster had not been discussed, and that the constitution of Northern Ireland would remain unchanged, but his remarks on the B Specials gave rise to speculation—not discouraged by subsequent Whitehall leaks—that the auxiliary force was to be disarmed and disbanded. Both sides, he said, wanted to see the B Specials phased out. "They are already out of the areas where the British troops are, and they will be phased away from the riot areas, which is not where they ought to be. Their disarming is a matter entirely for the G.O.C. It is his responsibility, and I think we can safely leave it to him."

Returning to Northern Ireland, Chichester-Clark was faced with rumbling discontent in the Unionist Party. Two former ministers, William Craig and Harry West, who had both been

dismissed during O'Neill's premiership, at first predicted the
Government would be called upon to resign. The Rev. Ian
Paisley said: "Mr Wilson has capitulated to the hierarchy of
the Roman Catholic Church by destroying at a stroke of the
pen the Special Constabulary—Ulster loyalists' last line of
defence." Frank Gogarty, chairman of the Northern Ireland
Civil Rights Association, was dissatisfied with Wilson's statement, and said: "We still believe that this Government—the
Stormont Government—has no moral right to continue in
office and that it should be suspended." On the whole, though,
the Unionists' critics welcomed the greater participation of the
British Government.

Significantly, it was Brian Faulkner, the Government's most
adept spokesman, who took the Press conference at Stormont
on Wednesday. He insisted: "There is absolutely no change
in the constitutional position of Northern Ireland and no
diminution of the powers of the Northern Ireland Government,
and the British Government has made it very clear that the
border was not an issue in the talks." And he added: "There
is absolutely no suggestion that the Ulster Special Constabulary
should be disbanded." The Prime Minister gave similar assurances to Unionist backbenchers later in the day, and a split
in the party was avoided. Craig said afterwards that it seemed
Prime Minister Wilson was indulging in some *Tiger* double-
talk, and that Chichester-Clark had not conceded any control
of the R.U.C. or Specials. "As soon as the rule of law is restored,
the Army will withdraw. The Government holds the real power.
The Army has come to its assistance to restore law and order."

Whitehall sources, however, were indicating clearly that the
British Government anticipated that the B Specials, while they
might not be disbanded, would soon be altered out of all
recognition. A word commonly used was "defanged", and
immediate plans were considered for bringing under central
control the arms of B Specials in Belfast and Londonderry.
It was recognised that rural areas presented a different problem, and that there might be no alternative to allowing the
Specials in such areas to keep their arms at home. A good deal

of importance was clearly attached to the Hunt committee and whatever recommendations it might make for reorganising the civilian security forces.

Meanwhile, the Republic's attempt to have its request for an international peace-keeping force placed on the agenda of the United Nations Security Council had failed. However, Dr Hillery had the opportunity to state his case during the procedural arguments. He asserted that the breakdown of law and order in Northern Ireland and the plight of the Catholic population was due to the partition of Ireland, which was brought about by an Act of the British Parliament for which not a single Irish vote had been cast. "The claim of the Irish nation to control the totality of Ireland has been asserted over centuries by successive generations of Irish men and women," he said, "and it is one which no spokesman for the Irish nation could ever renounce."

For the United Kingdom, Lord Caradon argued that the United Nations was not authorised to intervene in "matters which are essentially within the jurisdiction of any member state". The Irish application was adjourned, and Hillery said later that he saw no prospect of a United Nations peace-keeping force. There was no doubt, though, that Northern Ireland had become an embarrassment to the British Government internationally. Relations between Dublin and London remained good, although the Irish Government embarked on a campaign to publicise its views and strengthened its diplomatic missions abroad by attaching to them experienced public relations men drawn from semi-state companies such as Aer Lingus and Bord Failte.

On Friday, 22 August, the B Specials began handing in their arms in Belfast and Londonderry. General Freeland said: "I must emphasise they are not being disarmed. Their weapons are being brought under control, just as the weapons of the Army and the T.A.V.R. are under control." By this time, there were no Specials on duty in the streets of the two cities, although some remained on guard duty in the Belfast docks and at vulnerable points. They would not be used to man the border with the Republic. General Freeland said that, at the height of the emergency, some 4,000 of the 8,400 Specials had been on duty at any one time, but by 20 August the figure had fallen to 500, of whom 300 were in country areas.

From Stormont Castle came an announcement that the Government proposed to establish a Community Relations Board. Legislation would be introduced as soon as Parliament resumed, and it was hoped that the board would be constituted before the end of the year. The British Ambassador to Denmark, Oliver Wright, was named as the British civil servant who would be attached to Prime Minister Chichester-Clark's office; during the Rhodesian crisis, he had gone to Pretoria and Salisbury on missions for Harold Wilson. An assistant secretary in the police department of the Home Office, Alec Baker, was named to the office of the Minister of Home Affairs.

In the days following the Downing Street meeting, right-wing Protestants became more and more restive. Paisley accused the Minister of Development of lying and acting irresponsibly. "Faulkner should tell the truth," he said. "The B Specials will be destroyed and our line of defence with it." He suggested that some workers might hold token strikes in protest against the Downing Street settlement. An even more menacing Protestant spokesman had emerged in the chairman of the recently formed Shankill Defence Association, John McKeague. He boasted that his members had literally hundreds of guns—and rich friends if they needed more. "From now on we, the Protestants of the country, are going to take the initiative." Major Ronald Bunting, the self-styled commandant of the Loyal Citizens of Ulster, said: "The Protestant dog can bark, the Protestant dog has teeth, and the Protestant dog will bite if need be."

On Saturday, 23 August, Paisley planned a motorcade to Stormont, but he was warned that the Attorney-General had ruled this would infringe the ban on public processions. A number of cars then made their way individually to Stormont, where Paisley talked for an hour with the Minister of Education, Captain William Long, and said that Ulster loyalists would not tolerate the disbanding or disarming of the B Specials. It was a measure of the Government's deference to Paisley that a minister spent a Saturday afternoon receiving him; Paisley planned to lodge a second protest at Army headquarters in Lisburn, Co. Antrim, but was refused permission to enter.

That night, the Roman Catholic Primate, Cardinal William Conway, and the five Northern bishops, issued a strongly worded statement on the disorders in Belfast and Derry. It said:

> They deeply regret that the true picture of these events has been greatly obscured by official statements and by the character of the coverage given in certain influential news media. The fact is that on Thursday and Friday of last week the Catholic districts of Falls and Ardoyne were invaded by mobs equipped with machine-guns and other firearms. A community which was virtually defenceless was swept by gunfire and streets of Catholic homes were systematically set on fire. We entirely reject the hypothesis that the origin of last week's tragedy was an armed insurrection. We believe that a necessary precondition to any restoration of confidence on the part of the Catholic community must be an open recognition of these facts. In this context we regret that the full evidence available regarding the actions of some members of the police, in the early hours of the morning in the Bogside area of Derry last January, has never been made public. . . . The future can hold out no hope whatever unless the whole community is able to trust the forces of law and order.

Chichester-Clark's immediate reply was noticeably more conciliatory than anything he had said so far. He welcomed an appeal for calm contained in the bishops' statement, and said: "All of us believe we know some of the facts, but can any of us at this stage be sure that we know all the facts?" Some Protestants were critical of the bishops' statement, arguing that it would increase tension, but it seemed a proper counter-balance to earlier Government pronouncements.

Parliament was recalled on Wednesday, 27 August, to approve the setting up of a tribunal of inquiry. Chichester-Clark named a British High Court judge, Sir Leslie Scarman, as chairman. The other two members were Ulster businessmen with legal qualifications: William Marshall, a Protestant, and George Lavery, a Catholic. The tribunal was to be constituted under the Tribunals of Inquiry (Evidence) Act of 1921, which gave it power to compel the attendance of witnesses. It thus had wider powers than the Cameron Commission, appointed in March to investigate the causes and circumstances of sporadic outbreaks of violence and civil disturbance on and since 5 October. The Scarman tribunal was asked to investigate not merely the disorders which had occurred during August, but also a number of earlier incidents dating back to March. These included explosions at water and electricity installations, and petrol bomb attacks on a number of post offices in Belfast. Only one member of the Opposition was in the Commons to hear the Prime Minister's announcement.

Meanwhile, the Home Secretary had arrived in Northern Ireland. "I am not here to solve your problems," he said at the airport. "It is up to you to decide if you can live together in freedom and without discrimination. I will put myself at your disposal to help towards this aim, but it is up to you to find a permanent solution." Callaghan was accompanied by Lord Stonham, who took over the task of receiving the many deputations which wanted to make representations to the Home Secretary. The three-day visit was to prove a personal triumph for Callaghan, who diplomatically emphasised that he was there at the invitation of the Northern Ireland Government.

He immediately repeated the assurance that the border was not an issue. "It is certainly well known in the South—I have many friends among members of the Government in the South —you cannot change the border by force and, as far as the Parliament of Westminster is concerned, the border remains as long as the people and Parliament of Northern Ireland want it to remain." But there were implicit criticisms of the Government at Stormont. "I am quite clear that there are real fears and feelings of injustice and grievances, and feelings of discrimination, held by a number of people in Northern Ireland.

This fear is genuine, and no society can be stable unless these fears are examined and, if they are found to be true, remove them and ensure fair play all round." He said there were too many firearms in Northern Ireland, and that it was necessary to create conditions to ensure that the police force was accepted and respected.

Callaghan spent the afternoon touring the Falls and Shankill, and was often swept away from his bodyguards as enthusiastic residents tried to speak to him or merely shake his hand. He was greeted by placards saying "Only Catholic Homes Burned" and "We Do Not Burn Our Neighbours", and had an opportunity to see where the bulk of the damage had been done. He was shown walls pockmarked with bullet-holes. In Bombay Street, amid the rubble of burned-out houses, he had a demonstration of the Catholics' hostility towards the police when a plain clothes detective was recognised and had to be escorted through an angry crowd by vigilantes. At night, the Home Secretary held an informal dinner party at his hotel, with perhaps the most variegated guest-list Northern Ireland had ever known. It included Cardinal Conway and Sir George Clark, former Imperial Grand Master of the Orange Order; Westminster M.P.s Gerry Fitt, Republican Labour, and Robin Chichester-Clark, the Premier's brother; Nationalist leader Eddie McAteer and the Minister of Commerce, Roy Bradford. Cardinal Conway was to return for breakfast the following morning, accompanied by the Bishop of Down and Connor. The first practical outcome of the visit, which followed a meeting with the Northern Ireland Cabinet late in the afternoon, was an announcement that Callaghan would send a team of experts to investigate the effects of CS tearsmoke in Derry.

The Government of the Republic continued to be preoccupied with the Northern situation. A week before, it had criticised the Downing Street talks because they had "produced very little which would effectively contribute to a solution for the political, social and economic injustices from which the minority in the Six Counties has suffered so grievously and for so long". A statement from Dublin had claimed that the constitutional position of the Northern Ireland Government had already been altered in that control of the police forces had passed from the civil power at Stormont to the British military authorities controlled by Westminster. Now there came a reply from Lynch to Callaghan's statement that the border was not an issue.

> The Government reiterates its conviction that the unnatural partition of Ireland is basic to the present unrest in the Six Counties and that no long-term, much less a permanent solution can be contemplated without having full regard to its existence. . . . There can be no return to the status quo. Distrust and fear must be banished and the barriers of suspicion and prejudice must be removed. That this is possible is illustrated by the fact that people of all religions can live as equals in peace and friendship with each other in this part of the country and that the religious minority have no fears whatsoever of any discrimination against them.

Lynch said his Government was willing to discuss with the British Government the possibility of a solution along federal lines.

The following day, having talked to Rev. Ian Paisley, Callaghan visited Bogside. For almost half an hour, he was engulfed in a turbulent crowd, and ultimately had to take shelter in a house. When the Home Secretary passed through the barricades, he left behind his military escort and put himself in the hands of Bogside's leaders and two Independent M.P.s, John Hume and Ivan Cooper. From the beginning, demonstrators chanted slogans, including "Special Powers go, or Callaghan go". Most of the tricolours had been taken down, but there was no doubt that many Bogsiders were hostile to him as a British minister. But more were anxious to touch him and shake his hand. It was a confused scene, but perhaps a fair symbol of the whole confused situation in Northern Ireland.

Hume spoke to the crowd from the house in Lecky Road where the Home Secretary rested. "Mr Callaghan has not seen the ordinary Bogside people he came to see. When he leaves, you can give him the true Bogside welcome." After an hour, in which he sipped tea and listened to local leaders, the Home Secretary appeared at an upstairs window with a loud-hailer. "I cannot pretend to find a solution overnight, but I will try to ensure there is justice and absence of fear and lack of discrimination in this country," he told the silent crowd. "I ask you to give me an opportunity for discussions of these matters in order to find solutions. I have said that I am not neutral. I am on the side of all people who are deprived of justice. . . . I would be deeply grateful if you would let me walk through Bogside."

Callaghan then walked back to the barricades, and visited a Protestant area, where he delivered a not dissimilar speech to a much smaller crowd. "What we must do is to work together to ensure that the fear, which is real, is dispelled." From the Protestants came shouts that they were not afraid. That night, a number of the detainees held under the Special Powers Act were released. Four appeared in court on criminal charges on Friday, but by the time Callaghan left Belfast on Friday evening there were no detainees under the Act.

Friday, 29 August, was the final day of Callaghan's visit. He met members of the Nationalist Party—"The smell of the burning fire is still in his nose after his visit to Derry," said Eddie McAteer—and then talked to Unionist backbenchers. The afternoon was taken up with talks with the Cabinet at Stormont. A final Press conference at his hotel completed the Home Secretary's visit. No member of the Northern Ireland Government was present as Callaghan announced the terms of a communiqué.

The communiqué maintained the polite fiction that the initiative for reform rested with the Northern Ireland Government, but it was clear from the new measures which emerged that Callaghan had substantially increased the British Government's oversight of Stormont. Joint working parties of officials of the two Governments were to examine how far Stormont's present practice or pledged commitments adequately ensured (1) the fair allocation of houses by public authorities; (2) the avoidance of any discrimination in any form of public employment; and (3) the promotion of good community relations by methods including the prohibition of incitement to religious hatred. They were to report within a matter of weeks. Callaghan also announced that half the members of the new Community Relations Board would be Protestant and half Catholic (a step without precedent in public bodies in Northern Ireland), and that a Minister with special responsibilities for community relations would be designated. It was agreed there was a need to ensure effective means of investigating grievances against public bodies, and of achieving redress if conciliation procedures proved ineffective. In addition, there had to be proper representation of minorities at the elected levels of government, by fair electoral practices, and at nominated or appointed levels by a recognition "that such minorities have a right to an effective voice in affairs". A mission from the Ministry of Technology, the Board of Trade and the Department of Economic Affairs would visit Northern Ireland to assess economic and industrial prospects. Callaghan himself would return to Belfast in mid-October.

"It is my view," the Home Secretary said, "that if these matters are pursued with energy and sincerity, this day shall see the beginning of a new era in the creation of confidence in the communities of Northern Ireland. . . . Now we have got to ask the leaders of all the communities to encourage their supporters and their followers and their flocks, whoever they may be, to give the opportunity, to give the breathing space necessary to translate this work into action." He repeated the pledge on Northern Ireland's constitutional position, and added "I cannot believe that the abolition of Stormont, whilst it may satisfy one section of the community, would reassure anybody else. So Stormont must stay. To attempt to get rid of it would heighten tension, not lessen it. It would create fears, not remove them." Callaghan appealed for the barricades to come down and finally, answering a question on whether he was prepared to consider a federal solution to the Irish problem, said: "I do not ask to see the distant scene. One step enough for me."

The term "breathing space" was to be heard many times in the days that followed, and moderate opinion in Northern Ireland clearly believed that the Home Secretary's visit had opened up a prospect of achieving peace. Cardinal Conway spoke of a "new deal" for the Catholic minority, and said: "This breathing space is vitally important. A further outbreak of violence could have consequences too horrible to contemplate. . . . It is the duty of all moderately minded people, and they are the overwhelming majority here, to make sure that it is their influence that predominates." But the roots of violence stretched deep into history—deep into the year of the civil rights campaign, the half-century of Unionist rule, the troubled centuries of Anglo-Irish conflict. Could the past really be exorcised?

2. The October Revolution

It began also on 5 October 1968—with another march in Londonderry. Four months earlier, Austin Currie, the Nationalist M.P. for East Tyrone, had squatted briefly in a house in Caledon which Dungannon rural council had allocated to a 19-year-old unmarried Protestant girl; she was secretary to the local councillor's solicitor, a Unionist parliamentary candidate living in Armagh. The Dungannon-based Campaign for Social Justice then asked the Northern Ireland Civil Rights Association to stage a march from Coalisland to Market Square, Dungannon, on 24 August. Police re-routed the march, when a Protestant counter-demonstration was threatened; the marchers held a peaceful and impressive meeting at the police barrier, beyond which at least 1,500 Protestants had gathered to prevent them taking their original route. The C.R.A. was then invited to stage a march in Derry, where members of Derry Housing Action Committee had been jailed for obstruction when they protested against lack of accommodation in the city. The chosen date was the first Saturday in October.

Derry was a discontented city. It had long suffered from heavy unemployment and poor housing, and many of its inhabitants felt the Government was deliberately inhibiting its development: one of the city's two rail links had gone, the new city of Craigavon had been sited in Co. Armagh, the province's second university had gone to Coleraine in preference to expanding Derry's own Magee University College. Despite the

Catholic majority in the city, a Unionist majority was firmly entrenched in the council chamber. The city was ready to explode.

The C.R.A. felt the 5 October march should be organised by a more broadly based committee, but the one that emerged had a strong representation of republican and left-wing socialist views. The planned route was from Waterside railway station, crossing the Foyle river by Craigavon Bridge, and through the city walls to the Diamond. This would have taken the marchers through areas traditionally Protestant, and the intention was to show that the C.R.A. was non-sectarian. However, there were protests from Unionist organisations, and the Apprentice Boys subsequently served notice of a procession on the same afternoon from Waterside station via the Diamond to their own hall for an "annual initiation ceremony". On 3 October, William Craig, the Minister of Home Affairs, banned all processions in Waterside ward (that is, east of the river) and within the city walls. The probable effect was to increase very substantially the numbers who took part in the banned march, and certainly it ensured ample Press and television coverage. Three English Labour M.P.s, Anne and Russell Kerr and John Ryan, flew in as observers.

On 4 October, the organisers of the march decided to defy the ban. The following afternoon, about 2,000 marchers assembled at the station. There were about 130 policemen to hold them in check, including two platoons of the reserve force —the riot squad—and two water wagons had been brought into the city. The local county inspector of police was on leave, and County Inspector William Meharg of the Special Branch was in charge; he used a loud-hailer to read the Minister's prohibition order. The police had blocked the normal traffic route to Craigavon Bridge, the route notified by the C.R.A., but the marchers suddenly decided to take another route along Duke Street. A platoon of the reserve force was hurriedly moved to the other end of Duke Street, and used their batons as the marchers approached. Two M.P.s, Eddie McAteer and Gerry Fitt, were among the first injured. The marchers halted, and stewards pushed them back from the police cordon. An impromptu meeting was held, and Betty Sinclair, a Communist who was then chairman of the C.R.A., asked the crowd to disperse. But some of the demonstrators threw placards and stones at the police, who were then ordered to draw their batons and disperse the march. It was a crude and brutal operation, made worse by the fact that police had by then blocked the other end of Duke Street and did not know the order to disperse had been given. The Cameron Commission, which was later appointed to investigate the disorders on and after 5 October, commented in its report: "There is a body of evidence, which we accept, that these police also used their batons indiscriminately, and that the district inspector in charge used his blackthorn with needless violence." Water cannon were also used indiscriminately, both in Duke Street and on Craigavon Bridge, where people who had taken no part in the march were sprayed.

There was more trouble later at the Diamond, where police took a banner away from a group of marchers. Fighting broke out, and police drove rioters down Butcher Street into the Bogside. A barricade was built and set alight at Fahan Street. Young Bogsiders threw stones at a water wagon parked in front of Butcher Gate. As the evening wore on, Protestant youths gathered on the city walls, and were stoned from below as they shouted party slogans. Young Catholics roamed through the streets after midnight, breaking shop windows. There was more trouble on Sunday, as demonstrators threw up barricades from which they stoned the police, who retaliated with batons and water cannon. Monday night produced new clashes, and petrol bombs were thrown at police vehicles, but the situation gradually eased.

Craig was quick to reject allegations of brutality against the police. On Sunday, he told a Press conference in Belfast that all the activities of the civil rights movement indicated that it was predominantly a Republican front. He said Cathal Goulding, a leading member of the I.R.A. in the Republic, had been at Derry; Goulding subsequently denied this, and Craig was never able to prove his assertion. In London, Harold Wilson asked Home Secretary Callaghan for a report on the violence in Derry. In Kilkenny, Jack Lynch said he hoped the root causes of such demonstrations would be eliminated, so that people of deep religious beliefs and political convictions would be treated as equals in every respect, and would be permitted to live with each other in peace and harmony. Partition, he said, was the first and foremost root cause.

The civil rights movement in Northern Ireland was of comparatively recent origin, although as long ago as 1936 the National Council for Civil Liberties had published a highly critical report on the Special Powers Act. One problem, which was to continue, was that it was difficult to develop a movement which was not largely Catholic in membership. Policies to which the civil rights movement took exception were, in essence, policies which maintained the Protestant ascendancy and protected Northern Ireland from attack by elements which were largely Catholic as well as Republican. Protestants who criticised the prevailing system were likely to encounter hostility in their business and social life, and to be accused of being a "Lundy"—a reference to the Governor of Derry who, in 1689, had been prepared to negotiate the surrender of the city.

The success of the civil rights movement in recent times stemmed partly from the fact that it concentrated less on issues of personal liberty—few people, in fact, experienced the oppressive measures contained in the Special Powers Act—and more on pressing social problems like housing and employment. The target was less the Unionist Government than the Unionist-controlled councils; Catholic resentment was organised, not for the traditional and seemingly unattainable objective of Irish unity, but towards clear social goals.

In 1963, the Campaign for Social Justice was founded in Dungannon by a doctor's wife, Patricia McCluskey, to fight religious discrimination in council housing. It was not immediately successful, in practical terms, but links began to develop between Northern Ireland and some Labour backbenchers at Westminster. Labour interest in Northern Ireland was further

stimulated after Gerry Fitt won the West Belfast seat at Westminster in 1966, breaking the Unionists' monopoly of the 12
Ulster seats. The Northern Ireland Civil Rights Association
was formed early in 1967, with a constitution similar to that
of the National Council for Civil Liberties, to which it is
affiliated. Its membership covers a wide spectrum of political
views, and is predominantly Catholic. It believes in non-violent
protest and agitation within the limits of the law, although
some of its individual members are almost certainly less scrupu-
lous; the Cameron Commission noted that known members of
the I.R.A. had been stewards at C.R.A. demonstrations but
had been "efficient stewards, maintaining discipline and check-
ing any disposition to indiscipline or disorder".

The Civil Authorities (Special Powers) Act was first passed
in 1922, then renewed annually until 1933, when another Act
made its duration indefinite. It provides for the delegation of
very wide powers to the civil authority, generally the Minister
of Home Affairs or the police, "to take all such steps and issue
all such orders as may be necessary for preserving the peace and
maintaining order". One section says: "If any person does any
act of such a nature as to be calculated to be prejudicial to the
preservation of the peace or maintenance of order in Northern
Ireland and not specifically provided for in the regulations, he
shall be deemed to be guilty of an offence against the regulations." Another section provides the death penalty for offences
of causing or attempting to cause an explosion likely to endanger
life or property, and another authorises whipping for lesser
offences involving explosives or firearms. The Act was the product of a turbulent period, and early regulations made under
it provided for detention without trial. Many of the powers in
existence as the civil rights movement gained impetus were in
conflict with the Universal Declaration of Human Rights, in
particular Article 10 (freedom from arbitrary arrest), Article 12
(the right to be presumed innocent until proved guilty),
Article 13 (freedom from interference with personal privacy,
home or correspondence), and Article 20 (freedom of opinion
and expression). Special powers have largely been used to deal

with the I.R.A. and similar organisations, but the Act was also used in 1966 to declare illegal the Ulster Volunteer Force, an organisation of Protestant terrorists. The civil rights movement also campaigned for the disarming and disbandment of the B Specials.

Grievances in local government included the restricted franchise, gerrymandering, religious discrimination in employment and housing, and the lack of effective machinery to remedy grievances. Northern Ireland had not followed Great Britain in introducing universal franchise in local government; instead, the vote was held by ratepayers and their spouses, while limited companies could appoint one nominee to vote for every £10 of valuation up to a maximum of six votes. This clearly favoured the Protestants, with smaller families and an economic dominance. With the addition of gerrymandering, Unionists were able to control councils in areas where there was a Catholic majority (for example Derry, Armagh, Omagh and Co. Fermanagh), or to convert a small Protestant majority into a substantial majority in the council (for example Dungannon urban and rural councils). In each of these councils—and, indeed, in many others—housing and jobs were allocated to the advantage of Protestants. On occasions, housing projects suffered because councils feared the electoral balance between Protestants and Catholics might suffer. It is fair to say, though, that there were many "gentlemen's agreements" whereby Protestant councillors allocated houses in their wards, and Catholics did the same in theirs. The politicians had rather come to terms with the inequalities of Northern Ireland life, and the intiative for change could only come from outside the existing political framework—and, as it turned out, in street demonstrations.

On Sunday, 6 October, a group of students from Queen's University, in Belfast, had visited Craig's home to protest about brutality in Derry; he called them "silly bloody fools". A meeting in the University subsequently decided to hold a march to the City Hall on Wednesday afternoon, passing through Shaftesbury Square, not far from the strongly Protestant Sandy Row. Ian Paisley then announced a meeting in Shaftesbury

Square, and had about 1,000 supporters there by the time the students began to march. They were re-routed by the police, then found that a group of Paisleyites had reached the City Hall before them. Police halted the march, and the students staged a sitdown in nearby Linenhall Street, which lasted over three hours. Another meeting was held at the University, and the People's Democracy emerged, with no restrictions on membership and no constitution. Its rules permitted anyone attending a meeting to speak and vote, and decisions taken at one meeting could be reversed at the next—or even at a later stage of the same meeting. It was an organisation which could easily be manipulated by a small number of dedicated activists. Eamonn McCann and Michael Farrell were the most prominent of these. McCann, who had been active in organising the Derry march, had been expelled from the University and had become a familiar figure in left-wing workers' groups. Farrell, a technical college lecturer, was a member of the Young Socialists Alliance, a militant group whose members had been present at the Dungannon and Derry marches. Also active at that stage was Rory McShane, president-elect of the students' representative council; but the president, Dr Ian Brick, warned that "all too often students are used as a readily available supply of people for others to manipulate". In the weeks that followed, P.D. organised meetings in different parts of Northern Ireland, often attracting the rowdy attentions of militant Protestants. The organisation also staged a sitdown in the entrance hall at Stormont on United Nations Day, 24 October, demanding that M.P.s sign a document in support of civil rights.

The Derry Citizens' Action Committee was also formed. It included representatives of the five local organisations which had helped to arrange the 5 October march, and eleven other individuals. The chairman was Ivan Cooper, a 26-year-old business man and former Young Unionist who had joined the local Labour Party. The vice-chairman was John Hume, a 30-year-old former schoolteacher deeply involved in the city's social and economic problems; he had given up teaching to develop a smoked salmon business, and was president of the Credit

Union League of Ireland, a self-help movement. Eamonn McCann was not a member. One member, a Unionist, resigned soon afterwards over a decision to hold a sitdown in Guildhall Square on 19 October. On 18 October, a new group called the Loyal Citizens of Ulster announced a simultaneous meeting on the walls overlooking the square, but Craig banned this and a dignified sitdown attracted thousands of peaceful demonstrators and warned of the growing stature of the civil rights movement. "One man, one vote"—an appeal for universal franchise in local government—became its dominant demand, and "We shall overcome" its song.

Meanwhile, the Nationalist Party had decided to give up its role as official Opposition, a role it had assumed after the 1965 meetings between Terence O'Neill and Sean Lemass, then Prime Minister of the Republic. When the Commons met on 16 October, Craig said the Irish Workers Group had been involved in the Derry disturbances and aimed to overthrow the existing Irish states and establish an all-Ireland socialist workers' republic. He named the group's leader as Gerard Lawless, and described him as a former member of the I.R.A. who had been interned by the Government in the Republic in 1957. (Lawless was also a contributor to the English satirical magazine, *Private Eye*, under the name of Sean Reid.) Eamonn McCann was described as chairman of the Irish Workers Group in Northern Ireland. Craig said that the Nationalist and Republican parties must carry a major share of the blame for the movement towards violence. "Perhaps the real reason for their absence today," he said, looking at the empty Opposition benches, "is that they know they are guilty." Craig also named Rory McShane as a member of the Irish Workers Group, and noted that he had been prominent in forming a Republican club at the University. McShane said later he had severed all connection with the group in February, and believed it to be defunct.

On Saturday, 26 October, a small group of civil rights demonstrators marched from Strabane to Derry, and were attacked with sticks as they passed through the Protestant village of Magheramason. McAteer commented: "I find it absolutely outrageous that, in spite of a clear warning by a member of the Citizens' Action Committee to the police that there was a possibility of an attack on the marchers, the police failed to prevent an ambush." On 29 October, a Nationalist alderman told the Mayor of Derry that his occupation of the mayoral chair was a personal affront to the vast majority of Derry citizens, and tried to haul him out of it. There were rowdy scenes and the secretary of the Derry Housing Action Committee took the chair during an adjournment.

On 30 October, Jack Lynch spent an hour with Harold Wilson in London, and repeated his view that partition was the root cause of the trouble in Derry. He told the Anglo-Irish Parliamentary Group at Westminster that "the clashes in the streets of Derry are an expression of the evils which partition has brought in its train", and drew an angry reply from Prime Minister Terence O'Neill, who spoke of a "quite unwarranted intervention by Mr Lynch into our domestic affairs."

Also on 30 October, the Queen's Speech at Westminster announced the setting up of a commission to inquire into the British Constitution, and Wilson commented: "The commission will need to take into account what may follow the talks with the Government of Northern Ireland. Many of these problems have great urgency and it is important that, while the deeper issues are being studied, Parliament must be free to act." Edward Heath, the Leader of the Opposition, asked if the Prime Minister still adhered to what he and Clement Attlee had said about there being no change in the constitutional position of Northern Ireland without the consent of the people of that country. Wilson replied that those were not exactly the terms of his and Attlee's statements on the matter, but the pledge they had given still stood.

Attlee, Prime Minister of the post-war Labour Government, had actually said on 28 October 1948 that "the view of Her Majesty's Government has always been that no change should be made in the constitutional status of Northern Ireland without Northern Ireland's free agreement". On 6 May 1965

Wilson told Sir Alec Douglas-Home that he had been a member of the Cabinet that made this pledge and stood by it. The Ireland Act of 1949 used different words, and affirmed that "in no event will Northern Ireland or any part thereof cease to be part of His Majesty's dominions and of the United Kingdom without consent of the Parliament of Northern Ireland". With the announcement of the commission on the Constitution, there was some discussion in political circles on whether the pledge referred only to the border issue, or to the convention that the British Government did not interfere in matters transferred to Stormont except with the Northern Ireland Government's consent.

On 2 November, the 15 members of the Derry Citizens' Action Committee breached Derry's walls, following the planned route of the 5 October march to the Diamond, where the United Nations declaration of Human Rights was read. There was token opposition from the Loyal Citizens of Ulster, led by Major Bunting in army tunic, who had been told by the police that they must put back a simultaneous demonstration for an hour. The following day, O'Neill flew to London, and was followed by Craig and Brian Faulkner, the Minister of Commerce.

The Downing Street meeting on Monday, 4 November, lasted five hours. Wilson was accompanied by Callaghan and Alice Bacon, a former Minister of State at the Home Office who deputised for the absent Lord Stonham. The talks covered five main areas: Derry, local government franchise, housing allocations, the Special Powers Acts, and the possibility of appointing a Northern Ireland ombudsman. The following day, Wilson said at Westminster that, if O'Neill or his ideals were overthrown by extremists, the British Government would need to consider a "very fundamental reappraisal" of its relations with Northern Ireland. He added that he was sure the Commons would feel more confident in the administration if the Northern Ireland Government appointed an impartial inquiry into the events in Derry. Brian Faulkner had said after the Downing Street meeting that the British Government would not interfere in Northern Ireland's internal affairs, but it was already clear that increasing involvement was likely. There were hints of financial sanctions if reforms were delayed, and Finance Minister Herbert Kirk spelt out Stormont's dependence on Treasury support at a meeting of the Unionist Parliamentary Party a few days later. O'Neill, however, resisted pressure for an inquiry.

The first practical breakthrough in Derry came on 8 November, when the Unionist-controlled Derry Corporation agreed to Nationalist proposals for the allocation of council houses on a points system. The following day, the city saw yet another demonstration—a march to the Diamond, led by Paisley and Bunting. Police baton-charged youths who threw stones, but there were no serious disorders. The city prepared for another civil rights march the following Saturday, 16 November. It would follow the original 5 October route to the Diamond, then down Shipquay Street to Guildhall Square. On 13 November, Craig banned all processions within the walls for one month. The Derry Citizens' Action Committee was served with notices re-routing the parade; east of the river, it was to follow Duke Street instead of Spencer Road, and once over Craigavon Bridge it was to be diverted around the walls to Guildhall Square. The committee held an emergency meeting, and said: "We are marching peacefully on Saturday over the route which we have announced." The Loyal Citizens of Ulster warned: "No placard-carrying Fenian will be allowed to pass through Derry's walls." The Churches' Industrial Council in Derry, representing the main religious denominations, appealed to O'Neill for a relaxation of the ban, but the Government stood firm and the Premier issued a call for "the exercise of the maximum calm and restraint". All-night vigils and prayers for peace were held in both Protestant and Catholic cathedrals in Derry. There seemed no way to avoid bloodshed.

But there was a way. The marchers set off in the afternoon, reaching Craigavon Bridge without incident. Just beyond the bridge at Carlisle Square, police had erected crush barriers, blocking every route except the approved one down John

Street. Behind the police, there were groups of Protestants, identified by red-white-and-blue ribbons in their lapels. There were close to 15,000 marchers, and they stopped short of the police. As the crowd listened to speeches, four demonstrators moved forward to the barriers. They cleared the first row of barriers, then moved on to the second, scrambling over against token resistance from the line of police behind. The watching crowd cheered, and somehow honour was satisfied, though a few stones were thrown as the demonstators moved into John Street, firmly marshalled by stewards. At the end of John Street, some of the marchers turned up towards the Diamond, and broke through an ambush of stones to enter the walled city by Ferryquay Gate. Later, they were joined by the main body of demonstrators, who walked unopposed up Shipquay Street from Guildhall Square. By the time the demonstrators dispersed peacefully, they had destroyed the Protestant ascendancy in the city; it only remained for the Government to recognise this.

So far, the Derry Citizens' Action Committee had controlled the situation very effectively, but there were sporadic disturbances the following week. Demonstrators chanted slogans outside the courthouse on Monday, when summonses against 46 people charged with offences on 5 October were adjourned. About 400 dockers stopped work, and marched into the walled city shouting "Craig out". Girls from local factories also defied Craig's ban. In addition, the Nationalist Party had met at Dungannon on Sunday, and agreed on a campaign of civil disobedience. On 19 November, the Minister of Development, William Fitzsimmons, summoned the Mayor of Derry and the chairman of the neighbouring Derry rural council to Stormont, and told them he was considering the appointment of a development commission to implement the area plan which had been prepared. It was clear that reforms were on the way, but no one believed that the Unionist Parliamentary Party would accept "one man, one vote". Finally, the Cabinet hammered out its programme, and presented it to a meeting of the parliamentary party on Friday, 22 November. When the long meeting ended, O'Neill revealed the Unionists' five-point reform programme.

(1) Housing: Local authorities would be required to allocate houses on the basis of a readily understood and published scheme, such as the "group plus points" system.

(2) Citizens' grievances: There would be consideration of the need for effective machinery, and in the area of central government an ombudsman would be appointed.

(3) Derry: A development commission would be appointed.

(4) Local government franchise: Once the Government had decided the basis for restructuring local government, consideration would be given to a review of the franchise. The company vote would be abolished at an early date.

(5) The Special Powers Act: The Government accepted that, while it must retain its freedom to deal in appropriate ways with subversive threats to the constitution and security of the province, the British Government should be put in a position whenever possible to comply fully with its international obligations. Consequently, those special powers which conflicted with Britain's international obligations would be withdrawn "as soon as the Northern Ireland Government consider this can be done without undue hazard". If the Northern Ireland Government considered it necessary to reactivate these powers, the British Government would enter the necessary derogation.

The Government announcement of the reforms ended with a pious appeal for peace. "Upon the basis of demonstrated and apparent fairness, the Government must be firm in ensuring that law will be respected and enforced. Any who now continue to disturb the peace and dislocate the life of the country will be exposed as trouble-makers, concerned not with change but with disruption." In fact, Northern Ireland still had a long way to go.

It was soon clear that the civil rights movement was not satisfied with the reforms. The C.R.A. described them as a surrender to the right wing of the Unionist Party, which had "so often expressed itself as unalterably opposed to granting the fundamental rights and privileges enjoyed by all other citizens of the United Kingdom". The Campaign for Social Justice was equally critical, and the Derry Citizens' Action Committee said it would continue the struggle for "one man, one vote". Within the Unionist Party, there were signs of stress. On 28 October, at an Ulster Hall rally, Craig said he could not see much merit in the appointment of an ombudsman, except that it would expose those who were making reckless and unfounded allegations. Forty leading figures in the Fermanagh–South Tyrone constituency, including the Duke of Westminster, issued a statement in support of O'Neill; some of the signatories were prominent in Fermanagh Unionist Association, which still had on its books a resolution of no confidence in O'Neill, passed when he dismissed a Fermanagh M.P., Harry West, as Minister of Agriculture in 1967.

Meanwhile, a newly formed civil rights committee in Armagh had arranged to hold a march through the ancient ecclesiastical capital of Ireland on Saturday, 30 November. A route passing through the centre of the town was agreed with the police; it was one which Nationalist organisations had taken in the past, and Armagh had traditionally been peaceful. However, the Minister of Home Affairs had banned a Republican parade at Easter—a commemoration of the 1916 Rising in Dublin—and there had been prosecutions after the ban was breached. Local Unionist and Orange leaders made representations that the 30 November procession should be banned, and Paisley told the police that his Ulster Constitution Defence Committee planned "appropriate action" in Armagh, following the breaching of Derry's walls. He issued a public call for loyalists to "take over the city". Major Bunting gave notice of three counter-marches through Catholic areas and partly overlapping the civil rights route. He described the counter-marches as a "trooping of colour and cavalcade", and named the three organisations taking part as the Tubal Cain Group (Masters and Purplemen), Apprentices and Fellowcraft, and Knights of Freedom. As the Cameron Commission subsequently commented, "It is obvious that this was an action which was designed either to produce a total ban on both demonstrations or, if that did not take place, to lead to such a confrontation between the opposing factions as would in all probability lead to an outbreak of sectarian violence." In fact, police served a notice on Bunting re-routing his parades through Unionist areas, and delaying their start. Bunting then called them off.

But Paisley, Bunting and their followers had already taken over, despite a joint appeal for restraint from the Protestant and Catholic Primates of All-Ireland, Dr James McCann and Cardinal William Conway. They arrived soon after midnight on 30 November, and remained in the Thomas Street–Market Street area, on the route through the centre of Armagh. Later in the morning, police set up road blocks around Armagh and searched incoming cars, seizing two revolvers and 220 other weapons, such as bill-hooks, scythes and pipes hammered into sharp points. The group in the centre of Armagh was now seen to have sticks and pieces of timber. Shortly before mid-day, District Inspector Hedley Buchanan called on Paisley and his supporters to disperse; he said that in his opinion they were an unlawful assembly, because they were armed and gave reasonable grounds for expecting violence. They refused, and continued to sing hymns. By 1.0 p.m., there were at least 1,000 Protestants blocking the route, and County Inspector Sam Sherrard decided the march would have to be halted at Thomas Street. The police put two sets of barricades in the narrow street, about 75 yards apart. When the 5,000 or more civil rights marchers reached the barricades, they eventually accepted the police decision, and were gradually moved back by stewards with linked arms. Sherrard told them: "It is my considered opinion and the opinion of other responsible police officers that it would be unsafe for you people to go any further." At the other end of Thomas Street, Paisley's supporters brandished clubs and screamed "Let them through".

There were some scuffles later in the day. Two buses bringing counter-demonstrators into Armagh had parked close to the Catholic cathedral, and some of Paisley's supporters—armed with sticks—were attacked by a crowd throwing stones. The police made a baton charge, and a B.B.C. camera crew complained of being attacked by the police; subsequently, there were successful claims for damages and personal injuries against the local authority. Throughout the day, reporters and photographers had been intimidated by the Protestant mob—an experience which was to become a familiar one in the months ahead. Another victim of the mob, ironically, was a local solicitor, Brian McRoberts, who was stopped during the morning when he tried to drive his car through Thomas Street. The mobs battered on the car with sticks, and he had to be rescued by police after he was knocked to the ground. McRoberts was Gerry Fitt's prospective Unionist opponent in West Belfast; it was his young secretary who had been allocated the house in Caledon several months before.

The events in Armagh had the effect of polarising opinion within the Unionist Party, and within the Protestant community as a whole. The liberal view was that Government and police had woefully failed to secure safe passage for a peaceful demonstration, and that militant Protestants had scored a victory which could only encourage further militancy. The right-wing view was that the Paisleyite demonstration reflected widespread discontent with the latitude allowed to the civil rights movement, which must now be dealt with more firmly by the authorities. In addition, Craig's Ulster Hall speech had given a good deal of offence to Catholics and to liberal Protestants. He had referred to "the difference between our concept of democracy and that of a Roman Catholic country such as Ireland," adding: "When you have a Roman Catholic majority you have a lesser standard of democracy". The speech was clearly an embarrassment to O'Neill, in his efforts to build bridges between the two religious communities, and the Premier told the Commons that he regretted "some of the tone—not so much the content" of Craig's speech. "The Minister has been living through a period of considerable strain," he said. "I have noticed him fairly tired lately. I think we must bear that in mind when we consider the tone of his remarks." Craig, who had a long record of verbal indiscretions, refused to accept the mild rebuke and said his speech had been no more than a firm, straight declaration of basic Unionism. He went on to repeat the speech word for word at another political meeting on 5 December. Two days later, the party's standing committee endorsed "by an overwhelming majority" the five-point reform programme. James Chichester-Clark, then Minister of Agriculture, said: "The Cabinet situation is as it has always been—united".

O'Neill spent the weekend thinking about the mounting crisis. His bridge-building policy was in jeopardy, if not irretrievably damaged. Craig was challenging his authority. New civil rights marches were looming; the People's Democracy was to make its fourth attempt to march through Shaftesbury Square on 14 December, while the Young Socialists Alliance had decided on a four-day march from Belfast to Derry shortly before Christmas. The Prime Minister decided to broadcast on Monday, 9 December, to the people of Northern Ireland.

"Ulster stands at the crossroads," he began, and the words were to be repeated many times. He reviewed his attempt to heal the divisions in Ulster, and spoke of a minority of agitators in Derry and elsewhere playing a part in setting light to highly inflammable material. "But the tinder for that fire, in the form of grievances real or imaginary, had been piling up for years." He spoke of firmness and fairness, and said: "As I saw it, if we were not prepared to face up to our problems, we would have to meet mounting pressure both internally, from those who were seeking change, and externally from British public and parliamentary opinion, which had been deeply disturbed by the events in Londonderry." O'Neill said he knew full well that financial and other support from Great Britain—"so laboriously built up"—could no longer be guaranteed if the Government failed to press on with a continuing programme of change to secure a united and harmonious community. A reversal of these policies, he made clear, would be as unacceptable to a Conservative Government as to a Labour one.

O'Neill went on to quote from the Government of Ireland Act: "Notwithstanding the establishment of the Parliament of Northern Ireland . . . the supreme authority of the Parliament

of the United Kingdom shall remain unaffected and un-
diminished over all persons, matters and things in [Northern]
Ireland and every part thereof." Wilson, he said, had made it
absolutely clear that if Stormont did not face up to its problems
Westminster might act over its head. "Where would our constitution be then?" he asked. "There are, I know, today some
so-called loyalists who talk of independence from Britain—who
seem to want a kind of Protestant Sinn Fein. These people will
not listen when they are told that Ulster's income is £200m.
a year but that we can spend £300m.—only because Britain
pays the balance. . . . They are not loyalists but disloyalists:
disloyal to Britain, disloyal to the Constitution, disloyal to the
Crown, disloyal—if they are in public life—to the solemn
oaths they have sworn to Her Majesty the Queen."

O'Neill said his main concern was to bring a swift end to the
growing civil disorder. He appealed to the civil rights movement to "call your people off the streets and allow an atmosphere favourable to change to develop". To those who saw
Northern Ireland's position within the United Kingdom threatened, he said: "Unionism armed with justice will be a stronger
cause than Unionism armed merely with strength. The bully-
boy tactics we saw in Armagh are no answer to these grave
problems, but they incur for us the contempt of Britain and the
world—and such contempt is the greatest threat to Ulster."

"What kind of Ulster do you want?" O'Neill asked, and
again the words were to be repeated many times. "A happy and
respected province, in good standing with the rest of the United
Kingdom? Or a place continually torn apart by riots and
demonstrations, and regarded by the rest of Britain as a political
outcast? As always in a democracy, the choice is yours." He
warned that if people wanted a separate, inward-looking,
selfish and divided Ulster, then they must seek others to lead
them along that road. "Please weigh well all that is at stake,
and make your voice heard in whatever way you think best,
so that we may know the views not of the few but of the many."

It was O'Neill's last triumph. There was an immediate
response from moderate opinion throughout Northern Ireland,

which pledged support in telegrams, telephone calls, letters and petitions. Paid advertisements in Belfast newspapers listed the names of people who backed O'Neill. The *Belfast Telegraph* published a coupon headed "Ulster's voice", and tens of thousands of readers used it to register support for O'Neill's attempts to heal the divisions in Northern Ireland. But Craig's voice was also heard. On 10 December, he spoke at a Unionist meeting in Belfast. "There has been much talk on our constitutional position and reference to Section 75 of the Government of Ireland Act. I think far too much is being read into that. I would resist any effort by any Government in Great Britain, whatever its complexion might be, to exercise that power in any way to interfere with the proper jurisdiction of the Government of Northern Ireland. It is merely a reserve of power to deal with an emergency situation. It is difficult to envisage any situation in which it could be exercised without the consent of the Government of Northern Ireland."

O'Neill dismissed Craig the following day. "I have known for some time that you were attracted by ideas of a U.D.I. nature," he said. "Your idea of an Ulster which could 'go it alone' is a delusion, and I believe all sensible people will see it to be so." Craig replied: "I have never argued anything of a U.D.I. nature, but simply the need to defend our present constitution, which represents the settlement made when our grandfathers and fathers made their historic stand." He added that there had never been any cause to suggest that Northern Ireland had used improperly its powers in the past or now, or would do so in the future. Craig went on to receive a thunderous reception when he reiterated his views at a rally in Limavady the same evening, but a meeting of Unionist M.P.s the following day endorsed O'Neill's leadership, with 28 votes for the Premier and four abstentions. O'Neill stressed that this was a personal vote of confidence; Craig himself left the meeting before the vote was taken.

The situation appeared to have eased. In Derry, the resident magistrate granted a Crown application to adjourn until May all the prosecutions arising out of recent demonstrations in the city. In Armagh, there was a similar adjournment of cases in which five members of a Co. Tyrone family were accused of possessing arms and ammunition on 30 November. The Orange Order had passed a resolution supporting the Government, and there were now to be no civil rights demonstrations before the end of the year. But the People's Democracy had announced that a march from Belfast to Derry would begin on 1 January. The decision to march was taken at a meeting during the University's Christmas vacation, when about forty people were present; it reversed a decision taken at a well-attended meeting during term.

Craig's successor in Home Affairs was the Minister of Education, Captain William Long, a phlegmatic 46-year-old Yorkshireman fond of pipe-smoking and fishing. He decided to allow the march, despite a warning from Ronald Bunting that the marchers should stay away from "loyalist areas" or face the consequences. It began as farce; as about forty civil rights marchers left Belfast City Hall, Bunting marched ahead of them with a group of his supporters and a Union Jack. The accompanying police kept the rival marchers apart and although the counter-demonstrators sang Orange songs and shouted "One Fenian, no vote", it was fairly good-humoured. But at a bridge on the outskirts of Antrim, the first town along the route, the marchers were halted by about a hundred of Bunting's supporters, one of whom was beating a Lambeg drum of the kind familiar at Orange demonstrations. The police were unable or unwilling to force a passage for the marchers, and there was a long deadlock before Nat Minford, the local Unionist M.P. and a member of the Cabinet, arrived. He told the police to take the marchers by tender to a Hibernian hall on the other side of Antrim, where they were to spend the night. The police took a circuitous route. During the evening, Minford arrived at the hall and warned the marchers not to attempt to go through nearby Randalstown. There was a bomb scare during the night.

Also during the night a group of counter-demonstrators guarded a bridge on the outskirts of Randalstown, but police made no attempt to move them. Instead, they halted the civil rights marchers some distance away, and insisted they make a diversion, which they did in cars provided by sympathisers from the area. They were followed by the Protestant counter-demonstrators, and in Toomebridge—a village with a strong Republican tradition—a flowerpot was thrown on to Bunting's car. As the civil rights marchers walked through the village, the banner of the Republican club of Queen's University was unfurled. During the night, a nearby memorial to a Republican hero of the 1798 rising, Roddy McCorley, had been damaged by an explosion. The marchers were then diverted from the Protestant Knockloughrim area, and passed a number of hostile crowds before reaching the village of Gulladuff, close to Maghera, where a mob armed with clubs had gathered. The marchers circled round Maghera by car, while over a thousand thwarted Protestants rioted in the streets of the town. Cars were stopped by the mob, and some were overturned; several people were beaten up, and many windows were broken. The police made a number of baton charges.

Friday was comparatively uneventful for the marchers. They had intended to return to Gulladuff and march through Maghera, but the police refused to permit this. The marchers then made their way through bleak mountain country, over the Glenshane pass to Dungiven. They were joined by local Catholics—who at one point tangled with pursuing Protestants who had come from Maghera—and at Dungiven there were about five hundred marchers. Just beyond Dungiven, police tried to re-route marchers, saying that a hostile crowd was gathering farther along the main road at Feeny. The marchers, who feared that they might be more easily ambushed off the main road and indeed that the police might even be diverting towards a hostile mob as had happened after Toomebridge, voted to keep to their route. They linked arms and, without meeting serious resistance, broke through the police cordon. Nor was there any serious threat to the march as it passed through Feeny and eventually reached Claudy.

Meanwhile, Paisley and Bunting had made an unexpected

visit during the afternoon to the Minister of Home Affairs.
Captain Long said afterwards on television that the meeting
had been very congenial, and neither of his visitors had threatened or hinted that their followers would cause any trouble in
Derry. He agreed that the People's Democracy marchers had
been peaceful until that afternoon, when pepper had been
thrown into the eyes of some policemen outside Dungiven, but
said—to the amazement of many viewers—that the Protestant
counter-demonstrators had been non-violent. Long said he
would allow the marchers free entry into Derry unless the police
told him they could no longer contain the situation. The
Minister also issued a statement appealing for the march to
be allowed to proceed peaceably.

Paisley and Bunting spent Friday evening in Derry, where
the former was ostensibly holding a religious meeting in the
Guildhall. Stewards carefully scrutinised people going into the
meeting, and one reporter who did get inside was subsequently
removed by force. Bunting called on as many people as possible
to be at Brackfield church at 9.30 a.m. "to see the marchers
on their way". The church is on the main road from Claudy
to Derry, and not far from Burntollet Bridge. Outside the
Guildhall, an angry crowd of Catholics had gathered, and
stewards of the Derry Citizens' Action Committee did their
best to contain them. But the city's large Christmas tree was
brought tumbling down, and Bunting's car was identified and
burned. Finally, a group of young Protestants burst out of the
Guildhall, armed with clubs made by breaking furniture and
banisters, and the two factions clashed violently, while police
and civil rights stewards tried vainly to disperse the trouble-
makers.

On Saturday, 4 January, the marchers breakfasted and heard
reports of the previous evening's events in Derry. They considered abandoning the march, but decided to continue and set
off behind police tenders and television cameras. There was an
unnerving silence as they passed a housing estate where opposition to the march might have been expected. Then, at Cumber
road junction, they were warned by District Inspector W. G.

Harrison that a hostile crowd had assembled on high ground ahead, and there was a risk of stone-throwing. County Inspector Paul Kerr reconnoitred the road ahead and returned to confirm that there were about fifty people on high ground ahead. For some reason, the police made no attempt to re-route the marchers, who decided to go ahead, keeping in to the right-hand side of the road for protection. At the head of the march were about forty policemen with steel helmets and shields, and in front of them some youths sang Orange songs. There were about five hundred civil rights marchers. They passed the danger point indicated by the police without incident, but could see through the hedge another group of policemen (without helmets or shields) moving ahead of them on the high ground. As the march continued, these police reached groups of young men armed with cudgels, who also moved along the high ground ahead of those on the road.

The attack began about half a mile from Burntollet Bridge, where a triangular field fronts the road for more than one-quarter of a mile. At the end of the field, narrow Scribetree Lane joins the Derry road obliquely from the right. Just beyond this junction, Ardmore Road joins almost at right-angles from the left. Beyond these is Burntollet Bridge, and to the left the ground slopes down to the Faughan river. At first bricks, bottles and large quarried stones rained down on the marchers; they had been delivered the previous night, and distributed in convenient piles. The marchers in front had some protection from the party of police, but those behind were exposed except for what cover they could get from the hedge. There were about a hundred and fifty assailants in the field, and they moved along parallel with the march; police moved among them without halting the attacks, but did draw batons to drive back some of the marchers who tried to come through a gap in the hedge into the field. The attackers wore white armbands.

More than sixty attackers were waiting for the marchers as they reached the junction with Scribetree Lane. They had sticks, crowbars and lead piping. Ronald Bunting was with them. On the other side of the road, another group of assailants hurled stones from Ardmore Road. Once the police vanguard had pushed through to the bridge, the marchers at the back were shown no mercy. Many fell, hit by stones or clubs, and had to be carried. Others fled down to the Faughan river; some were literally thrown off the road, a drop of about ten feet, and others were thrown into the river. Many of the policemen remained in tenders stationed at Burntollet Bridge while the ambush was under way, making no attempt to protect the marchers or arrest or disperse the assailants. Many marchers claimed afterwards that the police had been actively hostile. Civil rights investigators also claimed that almost one hundred of the attackers they had identified by photographs and eye-witness accounts and other research had records of service with the B Specials.

Some of the marchers were knocked unconscious during the ambush; many others were left bleeding and bruised, the women suffering as much as the men from the attacking Protestants. For many it was the end of the march, as they were taken by ambulance and tender to Altnagelvin Hospital, in Derry. For those who covered the last few miles into Derry, there was more trouble. Again stones were thrown as they moved through Irish Street, and again there was no effective police intervention. There was a further attack in Spencer Road, leading towards Craigavon Bridge, where a disused quarry provided a vantage point and where piles of stones had been assembled. Eventually, the marchers crossed the bridge and reached Guildhall Square, having been re-routed away from the city walls by the police. Their pursuers from Burntollet and Irish Street assembled within the walls and sang Orange songs. One of these, "The Green Grassy Slopes of the Boyne", became "The Green Grassy Slopes of the Faughan". In Guildhall Square, Michael Farrell arrived from hospital— the dominant figure in the march, he had been injured at Irish Street—and told civil rights supporters that he bore the attackers no malice. "I regard them as unfortunate, misguided people, the tools of evil men. We should never retaliate. They are our brothers, even though they are misguided."

There was more violence during the afternoon, after the meeting in Guildhall Square had dispersed, and running battles broke out between young Derry Catholics and the police. As the Cameron report later pointed out, the high level of unemployment among Derry's young people meant that large numbers were on or about the streets, easily roused or led to disorder; demolitions made bricks and stones readily available, and the layout of the streets made riot control difficult. As darkness fell, police cordoned off Butcher's Gate, overlooking Bogside; above them, Protestants manned the city walls. As the police were stoned, they made a series of baton charges, and water wagons were brought into action. Barricades went up in Lecky Road. John Hume said later that, when he and Ivan Cooper approached the police to ask them to remove the water cannons, they were told their heads would be beaten in if they came any closer. He said one policeman struck him with a brick at a distance of five yards.

Relations between police and Bogsiders had deteriorated sharply since 5 October, and there was now utter hostility. Violence continued through the night, and people in the Lecky Road area complained that they had been terrorised by police —some of them drunk—who had broken windows and entered homes to baton the residents. The Cameron Commission later concluded that, while the police had been working for long hours and were under great stress, allegations of misconduct were substantiated and that there could be no acceptable justification or excuse. One consequence of the night's events was an agreement that police would keep out of the Lecky Road area provided that residents could keep the peace themselves; it was the genesis of Free Derry. Another consequence was a police inquiry conducted by County Inspector Harry Baillie.

The march to Derry was the beginning of O'Neill's downfall. "Enough is enough," he said in a strongly worded statement. "We have heard sufficient for now about civil rights, let us hear a little about civic responsibility. For it is a short step from the throwing of paving stones to the laying of tombstones, and I for one can think of no cause in Ulster today which will be advanced by the death of a single Ulsterman." He described the People's Democracy march as foolhardy and irresponsible, but said it had been allowed to go on because "this is a free country in which people have a right—which ought as far as possible to be protected—to state views however foolish and ill-judged and untimely they may be, provided they keep within the law". But, while he spoke of "disgraceful violence, offered indiscriminately both to the marchers and to the police", the weight of criticism was directed at the peaceful marchers rather than the Protestant extremists. It was a statement which offended many Catholics, and may have lost O'Neill critical votes when he called a general election in February. There was further resentment of a Government statement, following an emergency Cabinet meeting, which said the point had been reached when "agitation is not just expressing a legitimate point of view, but is attempting to bypass and discredit the ordinary processes of democratic government". The Minister of Home Affairs was authorised to mobilise B Specials for routine police duties.

During the week, O'Neill kept a lunch engagement in London with the Conservative leader, Edward Heath. He took the opportunity to visit the Home Office, and briefed Callaghan and Stonham on the Northern Ireland situation; afterwards, he denied he had asked for British troops or police. He also appointed a 42-year-old Queen's Counsel, Robert Porter, as Parliamentary Secretary in Home Affairs "in view of the exceptional demands the current difficult situation is bound to make". A branch of the People's Democracy in Newry, Co. Down, had given notice of a parade through the border town on the following Saturday, 11 January. The route took in a traditionally Unionist area—"to prove that we are non-party and non-political", said one of the organisers, who announced their intention to defy any ban.

Ronald Bunting warned that divisions of the Loyal Citizens of Ulster were moving into position and would stay under cover until Saturday. He said that marchers would not be allowed into any loyalist area. Newry was different from Derry in that it had a substantial Catholic majority, and most members of the council were Catholics. Few Protestants were employed by the council, but there was a sizeable Protestant business community and most of the unemployed in a depressed area were Catholics. Relations in the town were good, and many businessmen signed an appeal asking that nothing be done to interfere with the parade. On Friday, however, police notified the parade organisers of a re-routing, and Bunting said he had called off his counter-demonstration. Within the civil rights movement, it was widely assumed that the police or the Government had made a deal with him, so that the movement might be discredited if it resisted the re-routing. The Cameron Commission expressed some uncertainty about what happened, but did conclude that the decision to re-route was taken exclusively by police headquarters, and that there was no intervention by Captain Long.

On Saturday morning, a broadly based deputation saw police authorities in Newry. The P.D. organisers were included, and they agreed to accept a re-routing if there were signs of counter-demonstration. The police put this proposal to their headquarters in Belfast, but it was not accepted. The local P.D. committee met, and decided on a token breaching of the police barricades. It was then intended to have a sitdown, when the marchers would be told that some public buildings in the town had been occupied. The organisers had none of the experience which the Derry Citizens' Action Committee had built up, however, and many of the 6,000 marchers were young and restless. There was little opportunity to instruct the marchers before they moved off along Monaghan Street to Merchants Quay, where the police had erected crush barriers to prevent the marchers turning left along the quay to cross the Newry canal further up river at Sugar Island. The organisers had difficulty getting through the marchers to speak to the police at the barricades and, by the time they were formally told they must continue straight over the canal, the crowd was very restive. The public buildings had not been occupied, and the organisers had no diversionary tactic.

Suddenly, there was an assault on the barricades, behind which was a line of three police tenders. The crush barriers were thrown into the canal and, while stewards tried to maintain order, the attack was concentrated on the tenders; windows were smashed, and spotlights and windscreen wipers torn off and thrown at the police, who watched impassively. Some of the demonstrators climbed on to the roofs of the tenders, and spoke of the civil rights movement's non-violent principles. The tenders were rocked from side to side, and finally pulled back across Monaghan Street and burned. In all, seven tenders were severely damaged or destroyed, and one was pushed into the canal; some attempts were made to use the blazing tenders as battering rams, but the stewards stood firmly in the way. The police had drawn their batons and wore steel helmets, but not until much later in the evening was the quay cleared by a baton charge. During the trouble at the quay, most of the demonstrators had moved on, and a meeting was held in another part of town. Michael Farrell was one of a group who finally occupied the post office for a period. The Cameron Commission said later that it would have been preferable not to re-route the march, but otherwise commended the police, endorsing the avoidance of a direct battle while the tenders and barriers were being attacked, and noting: "On this occasion the police showed that they had learned much about crowd control during the previous few months."

The Cabinet met the following week, and decided on the appointment of a "high-level and independent commission" to inquire into "the course of events leading to, and the immediate causes and nature of the violence and civil disturbances in Northern Ireland on and since 5 October 1968; and to assess the composition, conduct and aims of those bodies involved in the current agitation and in any incidents arising out of it". The 1951 Public Order Act was also to be strengthened to deal with counter-demonstrations, and to make it an offence not only to organise banned processions—as before—but also to take part in them. A Scottish High Court judge, Lord Cameron, was later appointed chairman of the inquiry.

The two local members were Queen's University academics: Professor Sir John Biggart, the Protestant dean of the medical faculty, and J. J. Campbell, the Catholic director of the institute of education. The announcement of the inquiry was a factor in the decision of a civil rights committee in Strabane to call off a demonstration planned for 18 January; Bunting had threatened a simultaneous motorcade. But Harry West said the commission could be interpreted as "a manœuvre by the Government to get support for further concessions which they are at the moment afraid to mention to the party who elected them". Craig accused the Cabinet of losing its nerve and abdicating responsibility.

On Thursday, 23 January, Brian Faulkner resigned from the Government. In his letter of resignation, published the following day, he said O'Neill had been aware that he had been unhappy about the setting up of the commission of inquiry. "It is, in my opinion, a political manœuvre and to some extent an abdication of authority, and is misleading to the parliamentary party." Faulkner said the essential was strong government capable either of gaining the confidence of the Unionist Party for a change of policy and introducing on its own initiative universal adult suffrage in local government; or of resisting the pressures being brought to bear on the Government. He said he believed the first course to be right, but in either case law and order must be enforced. The administration, he said, fell down on both the alternatives he mentioned. It was clear from the letter that Faulkner felt that the work of his Ministry—where he had made a success of the drive for new industry—was imperilled.

O'Neill replied with a sharp letter saying that, after 5 October, Faulkner had been a principal protagonist of the view that there ought to be no change under duress, and had not taken any intiative in recommending any measure to take the heat out of the situation. He described Faulkner's proposals as the alternatives of "doing nothing or of attempting what you must have known to be politically impossible, and therefore in practice doing nothing. Hobson's choice!" O'Neill added that

if Faulkner had on occasions given him the loyalty and support
which a Prime Minister had the right to expect from his
deputy, some of the earlier crises might not have arisen.

A second exchange of letters the following day heightened
the bitterness between the two men. Faulkner said that, as early
as 23 October, he had made it clear he had no dogmatic views
on the franchise. He said that O'Neill had told his colleagues
that a change in the franchise was inevitable—and would come
from the commission's report. O'Neill replied that Government
policy was unchanged, and that when the franchise was
reviewed all relevant factors—including any comments from
the commission—would be considered. The Premier also published the transcript of a television interview Faulkner had
given in America during an earlier leadership struggle; the
Minister of Commerce, asked about support for O'Neill, had
replied that policies were much more important than personali-
ties and that he would not be a member of the Government
if he felt he could not support its policies.

Over the weekend, the Minister of Health and Social
Services, William Morgan, also resigned. He said he had come
to the conclusion that there should be a change of leadership.
O'Neill promoted Robert Porter into Morgan's post and made
the Chief Whip, Roy Bradford, Minister of Commerce. Both
were on the liberal wing of the party, and this merely emphasised O'Neill's diminishing control over the right wing. On
30 January, a junior Whip, Joe Burns, resigned. There were
13 signatories—including Burns, but not Faulkner or Morgan
—to a letter requesting party secretary Jim Baillie to call a
meeting of Unionist M.P.s to consider a change of leadership.
"What they truly seek is a change of policy," O'Neill countered.
"I intend to stand up and fight, together with those who have
supported me in what I believe in." On Monday, 3 February,
two days before the parliamentary party was due to meet, most
of the dissident M.P.s met in a hotel in Portadown and later
issued a statement saying that only a new Government under
a new leader could reunite the party. "A general election now
would be an act of irresponsibility and would widen the

divisions among Unionists." That night, O'Neill announced that a general election would be held on 24 February. He accused the dissidents of rejecting normal party procedures. "They have thus taken the debate outside the parliamentary party to the country, and it is in the country that the answer must now be given."

While the political temperature was rising, there had also been some lively and even farcical courtroom scenes in Armagh. Paisley and Bunting were among a substantial number of people who had been charged with unlawful assembly in Armagh on 30 November. Unlike the civil rights defendants in other cases, they had objected to their cases being adjourned until May, and on 27 January the two men were each sentenced to three months' imprisonment. The following day, police called to arrest Paisley and take him to prison, but there was a scuffle and the Free Presbyterian Moderator went to hospital for treatment to a cut hand. There was further trouble the following morning when police had to force an entry to arrest Bunting in his home; this led to Bunting being sentenced, on new charges of assaulting and obstructing police officers, to a further month's imprisonment. Paisley was taken to prison the same day, but emerged after 24 hours on signing a bail bond to consider an appeal. Bunting came out later, and both men became candidates in the election.

In the 1965 general election, only 29 of Stormont's 52 seats were contested, a reflection of the normally static pattern of Ulster politics. This time, only six Unionists and a Nationalist were returned unopposed. The Unionist Party was deeply divided at constituency level. Only 10 of the original 13 rebels were renominated, and every one was opposed by an independent pro-O'Neill Unionist. So were Faulkner and Morgan, and following a dispute over selection methods the latter was prevented by a court order from describing himself as an official Unionist. New Unionist candidates believed to oppose O'Neill's leadership were also faced with independent pro-O'Neill opposition. In turn, a number of liberal Unionist M.P.s were opposed by Protestant Unionist candidates, with Paisley challenging O'Neill in his own Bannside constituency. Michael Farrell also stood against O'Neill, and Bernadette Devlin took on Chichester-Clark in South Derry; there were eight P.D. candidates, and Hume and Cooper stood as independents. The election was essentially a test of O'Neill's leadership, and his critics complained that he should not have called an election to solve an internal party problem, but the intervention of other candidates confused the issue in some constituencies and probably helped the official candidates. O'Neill himself was indecisive about endorsing supporters who lacked the official label though he remained bitterly critical of the dissidents. He also fought a poor campaign in his own constituency, partly because the party machinery was rusty from previous unopposed returns, partly because he was never comfortable in the rough and tumble of politics, partly because he chose to oversee the election battle from Stormont Castle.

The Unionist manifesto was described as "not simply a statement of policy, it is also a declaration of principle". It committed the party to working to heal "those divisions in our community which have so far prevented Northern Ireland from fulfilling its best hopes". The party also proclaimed the right of all citizens to equal treatment under the law, to full equality in the enjoyment of health, education and other social benefits, and to the protection of authority against every kind of injustice.

Overall, the result could be described as a victory for O'Neill, but by so narrow a margin that essentially his gamble had failed. Only one of the 10 remaining dissidents was defeated, and he had declared "unequivocal support" for O'Neill during the campaign. Morgan was also beaten, but Faulkner's independent opponent forfeited his deposit in a three-cornered contest. A number of dissidents had narrow majorities—Burns' margin was 115 votes, and Craig held Larne by only 653 votes against a popular local doctor—but they were still back at Stormont, and O'Neill could not draw on the support of three successful pro-O'Neill independents at a party meeting. The Prime Minister had also suffered a blow to his prestige in Bannside, where the voting was: O'Neill, 7,745;

Paisley, 6,331; Farrell, 2,310. He had survived, but without an overall majority.

On the whole, the liberal Unionists had done very well—Bradford trounced Bunting—while the right-wingers were struggling, but O'Neill himself had done badly. Admittedly, Paisley was a strong candidate, but the inference was that the public backed O'Neill's policies but felt that someone else might unite the Unionist Party to carry them out.

None of Paisley's supporters was elected. Nor were the People's Democracy candidates successful, although one came within 220 votes of a sitting Nationalist in South Down, but they did better than many people had expected and it was evident that the civil rights issue could wean Catholic votes away from orthodox Nationalism. The point was underlined by the success of Hume and Cooper, and in two other constituencies victories were won by men prominently associated with the civil rights campaign. In Derry's Foyle constituency Hume beat McAteer by 8,920 votes to 5,267, with Eamonn McCann forfeiting his deposit with 1,993 votes. Cooper's victory in Mid-Derry was as remarkable; a Protestant, he drove the sitting Catholic Nationalist into third place behind a Unionist. Belfast's Falls constituency was lost by the Republican Labour veteran, Harry Diamond, to Labour's Paddy Devlin; though Labour was committed to the link with Britain, Devlin had been a familiar figure on civil rights marches and was an ex-internee.

On 28 February, four days after the election, Unionist M.P.s gave O'Neill a vote of confidence. He had 23 votes in support, while Faulkner voted against him and Craig abstained. Ten other M.P.s had also abstained, in effect, by withdrawing from the meeting. They had tried in vain to have it adjourned, so that the views of the party's standing committee could first be determined; two of the new M.P.s were now committed to the anti-O'Neill line. A week later, the standing committee backed O'Neill's leadership by 183 votes to 116. His position was patently insecure, as he reshuffled his Cabinet, bringing Porter into Home Affairs instead of Long. It was Porter's job to pilot the Public Order (Amendment) Bill through the Commons in face of mounting criticism that it was a repressive measure; unwisely, the Government chose to concentrate on this Bill in the first days of the new Parliament rather than on reform measures. The Opposition took exception to provisions in the Bill which introduced new penalties for squatting on the public highway or for occupying public buildings, and at one point staged a sitdown in the Commons, singing "We shall overcome", after a Unionist attempt to curb the long discussion of the Bill.

Civil rights demonstrations continued, but there were growing differences within the movement over tactics, and some moderates complained about infiltration by extremist elements —not the Republican extremists, but left-wing socialists. An appeal judge affirmed the original sentences on Paisley and Bunting, and they returned to prison. On 29 March, a civil rights march in Derry followed the original 5 October route, and passed off almost without incident. Then, early the following morning, an explosion on the outskirts of Belfast severely damaged Castlereagh electricity sub-station. On 31 March, O'Neill attended the annual meeting of the Ulster Unionist Council; his leadership was endorsed by the narrow margin of 338 votes to 263.

On the morning of Friday, 18 April, Bernadette Devlin became the youngest M.P. at Westminster. The previous member for Mid-Ulster, George Forrest, had defeated a Republican at the 1966 general election. His widow polled almost as many votes at the by-election, but Bernadette Devlin (chosen as a "unity" candidate following discussions between different anti-Unionist forces in the constituency) was able to command the natural Catholic majority in the constituency. It was a stormy campaign, though, and militant Protestant crowds harassed the 21-year-old psychology student whenever she held meetings outside Catholic areas.

On the evening of 18 April, Porter banned a civil rights march from Burntollet to Derry planned for the following day. A statement said: "Information reaching the Minister has led him to conclude that, were the march to proceed, there would be a repetition of previous disorder and violence." The organisers accepted the ban, but on Saturday afternoon there was a spontaneous sitdown protest close to the Guildhall. Then a group of militant Protestants, who had gone to Burntollet in case there was a march, returned to Derry and raised the Union Jack at the Diamond. Violence developed along familiar patterns, and eventually police used batons to drive Catholic demonstrators back into Bogside. A night of rioting followed, and there were allegations of police brutality, particularly in the house of Samuel Devenney in William Street.

A new clash was narrowly averted the following day, after riot police had taken up positions within Bogside. John Hume persuaded residents to evacuate the area at 3.0 p.m. and attend a mass meeting in nearby Creggan estate. At 4.45 p.m., following negotiations by Hume and shortly before the Bogsiders returned with sticks and clubs, the police pulled out in exchange for an undertaking that peace would be preserved. The Cameron Commission was later to single Hume out for his "outstanding" work in the city.

There was other violence during the weekend. On Sunday morning, there were explosions at Silent Valley reservoir in the Mourne mountains, and at an electricity pylon at Kilmore, Co. Armagh. During the following night, fires were started at ten post offices in Belfast. There were explosions at water installations at Dunadry, Co. Antrim, on 4 April, and at Annalong, Co. Down on 25 April. During the week, the British Government agreed to send in additional troops, to help guard installations. The police reaction was to look on the explosions as the work of the I.R.A. or a Republican splinter group, but I.R.A. leader Cathal Goulding denied this in Dublin, and civil rights leaders tended to think that Protestant extremists were responsible. As with the Castlereagh explosion, the new disturbances occurred just before an important Unionist meeting. On Tuesday, 22 April, O'Neill told the parliamentary party that the Cabinet had decided to implement "one man, one vote". No decision was reached, and the meeting resumed the following morning. Eventually, the party carried by a 28–22 vote a motion "That this parliamentary party decides to adopt the principle of universal adult franchise at the next local government elections and will seek the support of the standing committee for this decision".

That morning, Major James Chichester-Clark resigned from the Government. He said in his letter to O'Neill: "I have been worried, not because I am against the principle of universal franchise—indeed I think it will come and right to come—but I question firstly whether this concession at this time will stop the activity in the streets, and secondly I fear that our supporters will lose all faith in the determination of the present Government." The standing committee meeting was fixed for Friday, 2 May, with a meeting of the full Unionist Council the following Monday. O'Neill clearly faced his greatest crisis and, amid suggestions of further resignations, there was speculation on whether he could carry on at Stormont if he was defeated at either meeting. On Sunday, 27 April, he called his firmest supporters to a meeting at Stormont Castle and told them he had decided to resign. Surprisingly, Chichester-Clark was there —and on him fell the task of withstanding the right-wing challenge.

On Monday, O'Neill confirmed publicly his intention to resign as soon as a new leader was elected. "A new leader, committed on his record of progressive principles but unhampered by personal animosities, may have a better chance of carrying on the work which I have begun. A commitment of equality and justice is binding upon every Unionist. I would be happy to leave this declaration as my political testament, conscious as I am that there is now no turning back from the movement it represents." O'Neill referred again to the Unionist election manifesto when he broadcast that evening. "It speaks in clear terms of justice and equality; it commits the party, in honour and in conscience, not merely to do nothing to enlarge the divisions of our community, but to work positively to end them. You will be watching, as I will be, to see to it that these pledges are honoured." He said there was one simple truth. "Here we are, in this small country of ours, Protestant and Catholic, committed by history to live side by side. No solution based on the ascendancy of any section of our community can hope to endure. Either we live in peace, or we have no life worth living."

O'Neill had become Prime Minister by traditional methods of consultation in which William Craig, as Chief Whip, had played an important role. But election machinery along Conservative lines had since been established, and there were two contenders for the succession: Chichester-Clark and Faulkner. The Minister of Agriculture and former Chief Whip had made little mark in politics. His father and grandmother had held the South Derry seat before him, but he seemed more the product of his years in the Irish Guards and as a dairy farmer on the family estate at Castledawson. Possibly this was to his advantage for, if little of his political thinking was on record, it meant that no one held much against him. Faulkner, son of a prosperous shirt manufacturer, was almost too well documented. He was much the most professional politician in the Cabinet, and had a notable departmental record in Commerce (the new industries drive) and earlier in Home Affairs (during part of the I.R.A. campaign). But he had sometimes seemed to be all things to all men and, if he had now assumed the role of reformer, the liberals distrusted him. Possibly he would have had a better chance than Chichester-Clark of carrying the party's right wing—and, more important, the mass of Protestants—into an era of reform without bloodshed, but he lost on a 17-16 vote. It was a victory not only for the liberal wing of the party but for one Protestant tradition over another: the landed gentry over Presbyterian commercialism, the big house over the linen mill.

Chichester-Clark's first task was to form a Government which could help to unite the party. Faulkner wanted to return to Commerce, but Bradford was unwilling to leave his new post, so he was persuaded to take Development. This Ministry gave Faulkner the explosive job of reorganising local government—but, had he refused to serve in the Cabinet, it would have seemed he was perpetuating the party's divisions. Three members of the "Portadown parliament" also came into the Government for the first time, one of them—John Dobson, by no means an extremist—into the Cabinet as Chief Whip and Leader of the House.

On 6 May, Chichester-Clark announced an amnesty for all offences connected with demonstrations on and after 5 October. More than 200 people benefited; Paisley and Bunting were released from prison. One effect, much criticised by civil rights leaders, was to close the Burntollet issue so far as prosecutions were concerned. Paddy Devlin pursued the matter in a long series of questions at Stormont, drawing from Robert Porter distinctly evasive answers. On 9 May, the Unionist standing committee endorsed "one man, one vote"; Chichester-Clark had now accepted the parliamentary party's decision on this, though he had resigned in April over the issue, and right-wingers dropped their opposition once they had toppled O'Neill. Soon afterwards, the Premier promised legislation to set up machinery to deal with complaints against local authorities.

On 21 May, Chichester-Clark had talks with Harold Wilson in London. He was accompanied by Faulkner, Porter and the Deputy Premier, Senator John Andrews. Chichester-Clark said afterwards they had made it clear they intended to revoke regulations under the Special Powers Act which were in potential conflict with the European Human Rights Convention as soon as this could be safely done. It would have been done already, he said, but for the recent outrages. Wilson, for his part, expressed a desire that the commitment of troops for guard duties at vital installations should be discontinued as soon as possible. Meanwhile, the Civil Rights Association had warned that it would resume demonstrations if the Government did not within six weeks indicate the timetable for its reforms.

There was minor rioting in the Hooker Street area of Belfast, off the Crumlin Road and along one of the frontiers between Protestants and Catholics. It began with the sort of incident which occurs outside many public houses at the weekend, but its growth was partly a consequence of the strained relations between the Catholic community and the police. On 8 June, stones were thrown at an Orange parade in Dungiven as it passed a Gaelic football match. A plan for a parade through the centre of Belfast on 15 June—to commemorate the Irish labour leader, James Connolly—was cancelled in face of threatened opposition from the Shankill Defence Association, and after police insisted on restricting it to the Falls Road area. Police had to protect four men who attempted to stage a symbolic walk along the original route. On 18 June, Opposition members at Stormont said that they accepted as reasonable the Government's timetable of reforms, while noting that the proposed reforms did not fully meet their demands.

Not everyone in the civil rights movement agreed with the Opposition members, and they were criticised by Eamonn McCann and Bernadette Devlin at a rally in Strabane on 28 June. On the same day, an Orange parade passed peacefully through nearby Dungiven, where the Catholic majority confined their disapproval to festooning the route with civil rights slogans. John Hume claimed that "a small section has deliberately chosen to attempt to split the civil rights movement at this crucial time in order to impose upon it their own political views". He refuted charges that the movement was sectarian and warned that the approach of People's Democracy leaders—who had called for strike action—was more likely to lead to sectarian strife than anything the moderates advocated.

There was an air of apprehension as Northern Ireland approached the annual Orange celebrations on 12 July, and Chichester-Clark was coolly received when he made a surprise visit to Bogside. About 2,000 civil rights demonstrators paraded peacefully over Newry streets which had been banned to them on 11 January, and Paisley warned that he and his followers would "take over the town" later in the month. There were demonstrations in a number of Ulster towns, including Armagh and Dungannon.

A new crisis within the Unionist Party was threatened: Faulkner had published his White Paper on local government reorganisation, proposing to reduce the number of local authorities from almost 70 to 17. Craig and West both said there should be far fewer councils—which would have increased the likelihood that all would be controlled by Unionists—while many Unionists engaged in local government feared a loss of power and prestige. Chichester-Clark cricitised "so-called Unionists who continue to throw stones at their Government", and the divisions of the O'Neill era remained. In addition, the Opposition looked on Faulkner's scheme as a new gerrymander, and there was resentment that Derry was to be confined to the smallish area controlled by the development commission.

It was in Derry that serious trouble again erupted. The Twelfth processions and rallies went off peacefully—except when a small group of civil rights demonstrators staged a sit-down in Dungiven—but the speeches were noticeably uncompromising, and the voice of the liberals was muted. One of the Orange resolutions passed at demonstrations throughout Ulster said that, while the Order stood for the undoubted right of legitimate protest, "we deplore political blackmail, intimidation and violence in the name of civil rights, and warn the people of Ulster against the totalitarian claims of the People's Democracy". Chichester-Clark, speaking near his home, attacked "Irish American bigots"—a reference to a campaign by the American Congress for Irish Freedom to dissuade American industry from coming to Northern Ireland, and to support for the civil rights campaign from Senator Edward Kennedy and other Congressmen. He also criticised people in the Republic for "the honours accorded to the bodies of two murderers—let us call them by their proper names—who in 1939 slaughtered in the heart of Coventry innocent bystanders and maimed others"—a reference to the reburial in Ireland of the bodies of two I.R.A. men. The Prime Minister spoke of deep resentment of the "unbalanced and malicious picture of the province presented to the world", but had little or nothing to say on Northern Ireland's real internal problems.

12 July was a Saturday, and after Orangemen had returned to Derry from the demonstration at nearby Limavady, gangs of Protestant and Catholic youths roamed through the streets

of the city. A fight broke out in the Diamond around 10.0 pm., and the youths of Bogside were soon stoning the police, breaking into shops along William Street, Waterloo Street and Butcher Street, and lighting bonfires with their loot. Paraffin and paint were poured across streets in the hope of igniting them as police vehicles passed. Barricades were erected, then removed by police who used their batons to drive rioters back. Violence continued through Sunday, and during the evening warning shots were fired into the air by a group of eight policemen who found themselves outnumbered and trapped in a back alley. Petrol bombs set a hall alight, and stone-throwing prevented firemen putting out the blaze. Passions in Derry were high, and they were heightened by the death on Thursday, 17 July of 42-year-old Samuel Devenney, father of nine children. Three months before, he had alleged that police batoned him and his family, and he had since been readmitted to hospital for a time following a heart attack.

Another man had also died. On Saturday night, a crowd broke into the Orange hall in Dungiven and ransacked it, breaking up the furniture. The crowd was dispersed after riot police arrived. On Sunday night, a mob attacked police who were guarding the hall, and petrol bombs were thrown and two police tenders set alight. Eventually a police baton charge scattered the rioters, but shots were fired in the town as people were leaving a Catholic dance early on Monday morning. Ivan Cooper later claimed that B Specials had fired 100 shots, but this was denied by the county commandant of the force. The man who died was a 66-year-old farmer and ex-I.R.A. man, Francis McCluskey, who was found unconscious at the road-side. He had head injuries and died in hospital; it was alleged that he had been struck during a police baton charge. The local Catholic curate said: "Let us be honest on this occasion. Almost all the violence was on one side." The weekend also brought disturbances in Lurgan, where trouble was caused by the display of a Union Jack in a street where Protestant and Catholic housing estates joined. In Belfast, Hooker Street pro-vided more trouble, and police forced their way into a public house when a tricolour was displayed as an Orange procession returned from a demonstration; some Catholics moved out of predominantly Protestant streets, claiming they had been threatened. As the pattern of continuing unrest became established, Robert Porter announced the alerting of standby parties of B Specials equipped with batons. Chichester-Clark cancelled the holiday he had begun in England.

The People's Democracy had planned to stage a 20-mile march from Newtownbutler to Enniskillen on Saturday, 26 July. It was opposed by the Fermanagh Civil Rights Action Committee because of the tension in Ulster. The route passed through two strongly Protestant villages, and Porter banned the march and any meetings along the route or in Enniskillen itself. P.D. members announced they would defy the ban by holding a public meeting in the centre of Enniskillen during the afternoon, but a hostile Protestant crowd gathered and after some scuffles demonstrators moved outside the town boundary and staged a sitdown on a quiet road, whereupon many of them were forcibly removed by police. Police had also arrested a number of P.D. pickets who had marched one by one through the town to the police station. There were 54 arrests, but it had been a good-humoured day by comparison with rioting in other towns, and the resident magistrate's decision to remand 37 people in custody for eleven days was widely criticised; in fact, 34 were released on bail on Tuesday following a High Court application.

The severity of the police action against a smallish group of young civil rights demonstrators in Enniskillen contrasted sharply with the police failure to control or disperse a Protestant mob which gathered at Unity Walk in Belfast the following Saturday, 2 August. There had been minor incidents as a parade of Junior Orangemen passed the flats earlier in the day, and a crowd of Protestants gathered early in the evening to ensure that they passed the flats again unharmed. Long before the parade returned, the Protestants were throwing bricks and stones into the flats, untouched by a cordon of police. There was, however, a running battle between police and the Catholic occupants of the flats, who hurled stones, bricks and bottles. There were more than 1,000 Protestants in front of the flats, but their numbers diminished after the parade passed, and late in the evening police used batons to disperse those who remained. Meanwhile, the Protestants who had followed the parade up the Shankill Road began to loot shops in the city's worst rioting for many years. Hooker Street again experienced violence, and there were a number of minor incidents, usually involving petrol bombs. There was more rioting on Sunday, as people on the Shankill Road put up barricades to keep the police out. One mob tried to attack the flats at Unity Walk. On Monday night, the police found themselves in a crossfire of stones and petrol bombs as they separated Catholic Hooker Street from Protestant Disraeli Street.

A statement from Stormont Castle warned that the Government would not shrink from "any measure, however firm or exceptional", necessary to end the disorder in Belfast. Troops were put on the alert. But Northern Ireland seemed to be firmly fixed in a descending spiral into more violence, and the week saw new trouble in Dungannon, as civil rights demonstrators occupied council offices in protest against housing allocations. On Friday, 8 August, Chichester-Clark and Porter had talks with Callaghan in London and discussed the possibility of using troops if the situation deteriorated. On Monday, 11 August, the Cabinet considered the Apprentice Boys' march which was to be held in Derry the following day, but issued no statement. Robert Porter called for dignity and restraint in the days ahead. In Derry, where bonfires blazed, crowds gathered and faced each other across a narrow road separating Catholic Bogside from the Protestant Fountain Street area. John Hume said: "We have done all in our power to see that no provocation will come from the people we represent."

3. *Protestant Ireland*

It began also in the seventeenth century. For England, the northern province of Ulster had always proved the most intractable part of the neighbouring island, and the Tudor conquest remained incomplete. Then Hugh O'Neill, Earl of Tyrone, made the mistake of taking the offensive and joining the Spaniards in an unfamiliar kind of battle in Kinsale in 1603. They were overrun by the English forces under Mountjoy, and the old world of the Gaelic lordships came to an end. In 1607, O'Neill and more than 90 of his leading followers chose to go into exile on the continent. The "flight of the earls" left a vacuum which was filled by the plantation of Ulster. Many of the native Catholics were expelled from their land, which was then granted to Protestant tenants from England and the Scottish lowlands, much on the lines of the American colonies. They brought a new way of life, with neatly planned towns and arable farms in place of the pastoral economy of the native Irish. Six counties were involved. Four were to become Northern Ireland's border counties: Londonderry, Tyrone, Fermanagh and Armagh; the others were Donegal and Cavan, now part of the Republic. The eastern counties of Antrim and Down, where there were large individual land grants, were excluded. Throughout Ulster, the native Irish were treated as an alien group assumed to be disloyal to the Crown. But many remained, on inferior land or in inferior employment, and nursed their separate traditions and their deep hostility. In 1641, the Irish rebelled against the colonists. Their leaders insisted that they remained loyal to King Charles, then in conflict with his parliament. Reports of brutal massacres of

Protestant settlers led in turn to reprisals when Cromwell landed in Ireland in 1649. Many more Catholic landlords were dispossessed, and the Protestant grip on power tightened. Later in the century, James II's accession to the throne raised Catholic hopes, but the king fled to France when William of Orange was invited to invade England and restore a Protestant monarchy. But James had a loyal Catholic viceroy in Ireland, and in 1689 he landed at Kinsale with a French army. Soon afterwards, a "patriot parliament" in Dublin passed an Act confiscating the estates of Protestant landlords.

The Orange Order was not founded for another century, but it is this period which provided its mythology. Orangeism's most familiar song, "The Sash My Father Wore", records the triumphs:

> It is old but it is beautiful, and its colours they are fine.
> It was worn at Derry, Aughrim, Enniskillen and the Boyne.

The Protestants withstood sieges at both Enniskillen and Derry. James was decisively defeated by William at the River Boyne in 1690, an event commemorated each 12 July by Orange parades. In 1691, the Dutch general Ginkel won a further victory at Aughrim, and Irish resistance collapsed. There was more confiscation of land, and a Protestant parliament began to pass penal laws to keep the Catholic population in a condition of permanent inferiority.

The Protestant ascendancy favoured the established Church of Ireland against the nonconformists, however, and eventually Presbyterians and Catholics were able to make common cause. The Protestant tenant farmers suffered much less than their Catholic neighbours, and in Ulster the system of tenant right gave a security of tenure and incentive to improve land that was absent elsewhere. But a rising merchant class in the North chafed under the restrictions England imposed on Irish trade, and in 1791 the Society of United Irishmen was founded in Belfast. It was inspired by the ideals of the French Revolution, and sought full civil and political rights for all. Its founder was a young Dublin lawyer, Wolfe Tone.

Belfast at this period was a lively city of 20,000 people; the linen trade flourished, and the city's businessmen joined in a number of voluntary organisations to promote education and relieve poverty. In 1784, when Belfast's first Catholic church was built, there were generous subscriptions from the Protestant population, and a parade of Volunteers—a Protestant militia—at the opening. It was a uniquely liberal period in the city's history, and it ended finally when the United Irishmen's armed rising failed in 1798. By this time, there was rising competition for rural land in Ulster, and Protestants and Catholics often came to blows. In 1795, more than thirty people were killed during a battle in Co. Armagh. Protestants met afterwards and formed a new society, the Orange Order, to defend their religion and their lands.

The 1798 rising was followed by the Act of Union and the abolition of the Irish Parliament in 1800. Gradually, the Protestants of Ireland gained freedom to trade, and Ulster became a thriving industrial region which was not so preoccupied with the agrarian discontent which afflicted the rest of Ireland. Even the great potato famine in the 1840s affected the North less severely. Within the Presbyterian Church, a long theological battle was fought between Henry Cooke and Henry Montgomery, the former insisting on rigid acceptance of the Westminster Confession of Faith, the latter arguing for greater freedom of conscience. Cooke's ultimate victory was a victory for Toryism, and he was principal speaker at an Orange rally in 1834 which cemented the new alliance between the landed gentry and the large Presbyterian community. Five years before this, the Emancipation Act had granted Catholics civil and religious rights. The radicalism of earlier years was now thoroughly in decline, and Belfast experienced sectarian riots for the first time. They were to become commonplace in the months of July and August, and Cooke found many Protestant clergy willing to join him in fomenting anti-Catholic feeling.

As early as 1843, a petition in Belfast called for the retention of the union with Great Britain or, if there was to be Home

Rule in Ireland, a separate parliament for Ulster. Northern Protestants, with a flourishing industrial economy, saw in the Union the foundations of their prosperity. Catholics, in contrast, saw the Union as a barrier to progress. Within the British Liberal Party, the advocates of Home Rule—in rather limited measure—gained ground. Protestant fears grew, and with them dire warnings of what papal rule would mean. Gladstone's conversion to the Home Rule cause was the signal for a renewal of the Orange Order, which henceforth attracted many more Protestants of substance and respectability and became an integral part of Unionism. The Home Rule Bill of 1886 was accompanied by riots of unprecedented ferocity in Belfast.

In January, Lord Salisbury's Tory Government was defeated at Westminster, and Gladstone became Prime Minister. Lord Randolph Churchill, who had lost office, wrote a few days later: "I decided some time ago that if Gladstone went for Home Rule the Orange Card was the one to play." In February, Churchill arrived in Belfast and promised the Ulster Unionists Tory backing. If Home Rule came on them, he assured a huge audience, "in that dark hour there will not be wanting to you those of position and influence in England who are willing to cast in their lot with you, whatever it may be, and who will share your fortune and your fate". He gave the Protestants a slogan: Ulster will fight, and Ulster will be right.

The Home Rule Bill was defeated soon after midnight on 8 June, despite a moving plea from Gladstone—"Ireland stands at your bar, expectant, hopeful, almost suppliant"— and the divided Liberals were soon out of office. But the riots in Belfast had already begun, with a fight between two navvies in the docks on Thursday 3 June. They were both dismissed— one a Protestant, the other a Catholic—but the next day Protestant shipyardmen swarmed into the dock area and beat a number of Catholic navvies with iron bars and other weapons. One youth who tried to escape to a barge drowned. His funeral procession two days later passed through the centre of Belfast on its way to Milltown cemetery, and police had to cordon off a hostile Protestant crowd in the Brickfields area separating the Falls and Shankill Roads. On Monday, troops of the Highland Light Infantry and the Northumberland Fusiliers helped police keep the peace in the shipyard and docks area, but in West Belfast a Protestant mob wrecked a timber yard and brick kilns belonging to a Catholic.

When news of Gladstone's defeat reached Belfast, many Protestants left work to begin celebrating. In the evening, police attempted to disperse a mob in the Brickfields, and after the Riot Act had been read police fired a volley of buckshot. There was worse rioting the following evening, and the Bower's Hill police station on the Shankill Road was besieged. When the police eventually opened fire, seven people were killed. The military eventually restored order. But there were to be more deaths before the summer was out, and ultimately a commission was appointed to inquire into the disturbances.

The general election on 6 July—which brought Churchill back into office—and the Orange parades six days later naturally stirred up passions. On 13 July, there was a confrontation of rival mobs in the Brickfields area, and two men died after police fired at Protestants who refused to disperse. Shortly after midnight, a policeman was shot, and one of the two escaping gunmen killed a soldier on patrol; the policeman died a few hours later. On Saturday, 31 July, Rev. Hugh Hanna—a militant Protestant whose voice had earned him the name Roaring Hanna—gave his annual outing for the Sunday school children of St Enoch's church. On their return from the County Down Railway Station, a crowd of young men and drunks met them and insisted that they march with bands through the centre of the city. There was trouble as they passed large Catholic crowds at St Patrick's church in Donegall Street, and the children had to flee to safety. Later, police tried to disperse a Protestant mob which had begun to loot a Catholic public house in nearby Old Lodge Road. They fired buckshot above the looters' heads without effect, then aimed directly at the mob, killing a 13-year-old boy.

The following Monday, 2 August, the Catholic parishioners of St Joseph's church also went on their annual outing. When they returned to York Street station, crowds of Protestants had assembled behind protective cordons of police and soldiers. As the children emerged from the station, the Protestants began to throw stones, and the ensuing riots lasted for several hours. Police shot one Protestant youth dead, and dragoons and infantry eventually cleared York Street. Trouble continued throughout the week, and a decision was taken (and later reversed) to withdraw the police from the Shankill Road and allow the more popular military to enforce law and order there. Police reinforcements had been brought in from the rest of Ireland, and it was commonly assumed that most of them were Catholics.

On Saturday, during another attack on the public house in the Old Lodge Road, police fatally wounded a young Protestant. In Cupar Street, a magistrate used firearms to disperse rival mobs. In Dover Street, police were ambushed and attacked by snipers, and killed three men as they fought their way out. Early on Sunday morning, shooting broke out in Cupar Street, and a young labourer was shot dead. Through the day, police had to deal with rioters in different areas and shot dead a number of them. Nine people died that day, and three others died later of their wounds. From that point, the rioting diminished in intensity, though the death roll still grew, and on 17 September three Catholics died in an attack on the police barracks in Divis Street.

The 1886 riots were the worst in Belfast's history, but they were not the last. Gladstone returned to power in 1892, and a second Home Rule Bill was soon on the way. A great convention was held in the botanical gardens in Belfast, with an attendance believed to exceed 300,000. The heads of the Church of Ireland and the Presbyterian Church led the convention in prayer. Thomas Andrews, a leading Liberal whose son was to become Northern Ireland's second Prime Minister, said: "As a last resource, we will be prepared to defend ourselves." Fred Crawford, a young engineer who was later to run guns into Ulster, had formed a Young Ulster Society whose members were required to possess a revolver, a Martini-Henry rifle or a cavalry Winchester carbine, together with a hundred rounds of ammunition. In 1893, there was rioting in the shipyards, and Catholics were forced to flee. The situation eased when the House of Lords defeated Gladstone's Bill, but there was serious rioting again five years later when the centenary of the 1798 rising was celebrated in the Falls Road area. Protestant mobs attacked the police who had protected a Nationalist procession, and public houses suffered as usual. The shipyards were again a trouble spot.

In 1905, the Ulster Unionist Council was formed, uniting the various bodies which had emerged to fight Home Rule. It began with 200 members, of whom 50 represented the Orange lodges, an alliance which in later years was to discourage Catholics who might otherwise have sought to join the Unionist party. Soon afterwards, the Liberals regained power at Westminster, but a more immediate objective than Home Rule was to curb the power of the House of Lords. It was 1912 before the Home Rule Bill was introduced, and by this time the Ulster Unionists were well organised. A Dublin lawyer, Edward Carson, had become their leader and in September 1911 he addressed a large rally on the outskirts of Belfast. Carson, the scourge of Oscar Wilde and the successful champion of young Archer-Shee, was an orator. He described the impending move towards Home Rule as "the most nefarious conspiracy that has ever been hatched against a free people" and said that Unionists must be prepared "the morning Home Rule passes, ourselves to become responsible for the government of the Protestant province of Ulster". The rally was held at Craigavon, the home of Sir James Craig, a whiskey millionaire who was to become Northern Ireland's first Prime Minister.

The liberal tradition was not wholly dead, however, and in 1912 Winston Churchill was invited to speak at a Home Rule rally in the Ulster Hall in Belfast, where his father had once argued the opposite view. The chairman was to be

Lord Pirrie, a shipbuilder who owed his peerage to the Liberals. The Unionists resolved that the meeting would not take place in that venue, hired the hall for the evening beforehand, and planned to remain there against any attempts to eject them. In the end, Churchill spoke in Celtic Park, a football ground in the Catholic area, after a group of shipyardmen had come close to overturning his car as he left his hotel. For the Unionists it was a victory, which they consolidated at an Easter Tuesday rally at Balmoral showgrounds, on the edge of Belfast. The presence of Bonar Law and many other Westminster M.P.s cemented the alliance between Unionism and the Conservative Party. Bonar Law made it clear that the Conservatives would not condemn the Unionists if they resorted to force, and later in the year said explicitly: "I can imagine no length of resistance to which Ulster can go in which I should not be prepared to support them, and in which, in my belief, they would not be supported by the overwhelming majority of the British people."

On 28 September 1912, thousands of Ulstermen signed a Covenant to defeat the third Home Rule Bill, which had been introduced at Westminster in April. It was inspired by the Scottish Covenant of 1580, and said:

> Being convinced in our consciences that Home Rule would be disastrous to the material well-being of Ulster as well as of the whole of Ireland, subversive of our civil and religious freedom, destructive of our citizenship and perilous to the unity of the Empire, we, whose names are underwritten, men of Ulster, loyal subjects of His Gracious Majesty King George V, humbly relying on the God whom our fathers in days of stress and trial confidently trusted, do hereby pledge ourselves in solemn Covenant throughout this our time of threatened calamity to stand by one another in defending for ourselves and our children our cherished position of equal citizenship in the United Kingdom and in using all means which may be found necessary to defeat the present conspiracy to set up a Home Rule Parliament in Ireland.

And in the event of such a Parliament being forced upon us we further solemnly and mutually pledge ourselves to refuse to recognise its authority.

Within a few days, almost half a million had signed. But what means might be found necessary?

Soon after Carson spoke at Craigavon, plans were laid for a Provisional Government of Ulster, and in 1912 the Ulster Volunteer Force came into being. Colonel R. H. Wallace, a solicitor who was secretary of the Grand Orange Lodge of Ulster, made use of an anomaly in the law which allowed two justices of the peace to authorise military exercises within their area of jurisdiction provided that the purpose was "to make them more efficient citizens for the purpose of maintaining the constitution of the United Kingdom as now established and protecting their rights and liberties thereunder". At first, many of the recruits used wooden rifles, but there were also arms from rifle clubs which had grown in importance since the first Home Rule crisis. Drilling took place in Orange halls and in the demesnes of large landowners. In 1913, Lieutenant-General Sir George Robertson, formerly of the Indian Army, took command of the U.V.F.

By various methods, arms were brought into Northern Ireland. The moving spirit was Fred Crawford, founder of Young Ulster, a single-minded Unionist who had once worked out a scheme to kidnap Gladstone on Brighton promenade and maroon him on a Pacific island. He had signed the Ulster Covenant in his own blood, and in 1914 succeeded in landing a large cargo of European rifles and ammunition at Larne. The Unionists' preparedness to fight had widespread consequences. Within Ulster, it created a lasting belief in force as a justifiable alternative to parliamentary processes. If Ulster could defend itself once, it could be ready to do it again.

In 1914, when it seemed that Ireland was moving inevitably towards bloodshed, the First World War put an end to the Home Rule question for the time being. John Redmond, who had succeeded Parnell as leader of the Irish Nationalist Party at Westminster, pledged his support for England. In the North, the men of the Ulster Volunteer Force were quick to enlist in the British Army, becoming the 36th Division. But the Home Rule Bill had gone on the statute book, and—despite negotiations—there had been no amending Bill to provide for the exclusion of Ulster. Inevitably, there was a sense of betrayal, and it was perhaps augmented when the 36th Division suffered heavy casualties at the Somme in July 1916. The men of Ulster had advanced against strongly held German trenches, crying "No surrender", but their success was nullified when they found themselves unsupported on either flank. The Army chiefs had blundered, and Ulster had paid the price; there would not be so many volunteers when the Second World War broke out. Northern attitudes were affected also by the Easter rising in Dublin, earlier in the year, which was seen as a stab in the back.

By 1918, when the war ended, the Home Rule Act had become an irrelevance. Sinn Fein, which demanded much more independence, swept the polls in the 1918 election and set up a national assembly in Dublin. In the "troubles" that followed, the British Premier, David Lloyd George, decided to impose a settlement which divided Ireland into two parts. Six of the nine counties of Ulster became Northern Ireland under the 1920 Government of Ireland Act, and on 22 June 1921, King George V opened the first Northern Ireland Parliament. A visible border separated Protestant North from Catholic South. Within the North, the Protestants had a two-to-one majority over Catholics, from whom they were separated by an invisible border.

4. Home Rule in Northern Ireland

King George V made a plea for peace at the opening of Parliament, which met in Belfast's City Hall. "I speak from a full heart when I pray that my coming to Ireland today may prove to be the first step towards the end of strife among her people, whatever their race or creed. In that hope I appeal to all Irishmen to pause, to stretch out the hand of forbearance and conciliation, to forgive and forget, and to join in making for the land they love a new era of peace, contentment and conciliation." He spoke in vain. Ireland was partitioned in violence, and violence continued.

The Government of Ireland Act was an unworkable compromise which forced on Northern Ireland a parliament it did not want, provided for a Council of Ireland which never functioned, and looked hopelessly to Ireland's two Parliaments eventually agreeing to yield their powers to a single body. The Anglo-Irish Treaty of December 1921 ended the war of independence and provided that the new Irish Free State should embrace the whole of Ireland, but within a month the Northern Parliament exercised its right to opt out. There was provision for a boundary commission to decide exactly where the border should be, but the Unionists refused to appoint a representative and the British Government had to do so instead. Southern political leaders were confident that Catholic border areas would be ceded, but in 1924 the *Morning Post* published a forecast indicating that only minor changes were contemplated

—and that the North would gain east Donegal, where there were many Protestant farmers—and in the ensuing controversy the three Governments agreed to the existing boundary.

Northern Ireland's worst sectarian violence continued until the end of 1922. The Unionists won 40 of the 52 seats in the election in May 1921, the remainder going to Republicans and Nationalists who refused to attend Parliament. Craig became Prime Minister. Outside Parliament, Catholics bore the brunt of terror, and learned to hate the B Specials, to whom were attributed many of the deaths and beatings which occurred. The Special Constabulary had been set up by the British Government in 1920—the A Specials were mainly ex-soldiers demobilised at the end of the war—and passed to the control of the Northern Ireland Government. The Special Powers Act was introduced in 1922. Almost 300 people were killed during the troubles, most of them in Belfast. Property was destroyed, people were intimidated and evicted, reprisals were commonplace. Catholics retreated into their ghettoes and defended themselves as best they could, often against Protestant mobs roused by weekend drinking. Joe Devlin, a Nationalist M.P., described the atrocities to the Commons at Westminster. "If Catholics have no revolvers to protect themselves, they are murdered. If they have revolvers, they are flogged and sentenced to death." But the Catholics, for their part, were unremitting in their hostility to the new state; the Protestant response was understandable, even if some of the methods were open to bitter criticism. Craig, it should be said, was a more tolerant man than many Unionists. He appointed a Catholic, Bonaparte Wyse, permanent secretary in the Ministry of Education and arranged financial assistance for Catholic schools. Another Catholic, Sir Denis Henry, became Lord Chief Justice.

Outside the law and order field, the Unionists took significant steps to maintain and extend their ascendancy. In 1929, they abolished the system of proportional representation—the single transferable vote, with multi-member constituencies—introduced by the 1920 Act. Joe Devlin, by now leader of the Nationalists who had decided to attend Parliament, described it as "a mean, contemptible and callous attempt by the majority which you now have to rob the minority . . . of the safeguard which was incorporated in this measure". Only the University consti-tuency continued as before. Both the Unionist and Nationalist parties benefited electorally from the change, and it was the smaller parties and pressure groups which suffered. Craig's objective was to prevent a multiplicity of parties developing and threatening the traditional divisions in Ulster politics. Arguably, the 1969 election called by Terence O'Neill might have turned out differently if proportional representation had allowed Protestants to choose without fear that a split vote would let in an anti-Unionist.

The Nationalist resistance to the abolition of proportional representation was partly the result of their experience of a similar change in local government. This had occurred in 1922, and in redrawing boundaries the Unionists contrived to gain control of a number of councils—including Derry Cor-poration—which the Nationalists had previously held. An additional consequence of the abolition of proportional representation, in both central and local government, was that many seats were seldom or never contested.

One other electoral change must be mentioned. Under the 1920 settlement, the number of Northern Ireland seats at Westminster was reduced from 30 to 13, becoming 12 when the University seat was abolished. Political life increasingly centred on the local Parliament, and the Westminster M.P.s' role was reduced. They became less important at Westminster and, with Nationalists abstaining for part of the time, the Unionists were content that Ulster's affairs were not often scrutinised. Indeed, it can prove difficult to discuss at Westminster matters in which ministerial responsibility seems to have been transferred to Stormont.

Potentially, Westminster's strongest control over the years has been a financial one, exercised in the negotiations between Stormont and the Treasury over the Ulster budget. The original intention of the Government of Ireland Act was that

Northern Ireland should be a self-financing region, but this soon proved impractical—in part, because the province had little freedom to raise revenue—and Stormont has sacrificed much of its parliamentary, administrative and financial independence so that necessary social and economic development could go ahead at the expense of the British Exchequer. The concept of parity with Great Britain developed, with the Treasury making the necessary financial provisions to implement this (generously in recent years, making arbitration by a joint exchequer board unnecessary). This financial oversight by the British Government—though not in any real sense ever examined by the two Parliaments—could be argued to be a precedent for more recent oversight in non-financial matters. Both the civil rights movement and James Callaghan have, in effect, pressed for parity to be extended over a wider area of administration.

The 1930s brought new sectarian violence, possibly a partial consequence of politicians' fear that the depression might unite hungry Protestant and Catholic workers. In 1925, a march of unemployed to Parliament was banned; a few years later, when hunger marches and other protests had become common in Great Britain, workers were less willing to accept a ban. So, in 1932, there was an outburst of rioting in the Shankill Road when unemployed Protestants were told that police were fighting their fellow unemployed in the Falls Road. Two men died, but the workers' unity proved fragile; the previous year, the Ulster Protestant League had been founded in the city, and its militant anti-Catholicism forced the Government to adopt uncompromising postures.

On 12 July 1932, Craig said: "Ours is a Protestant Government and I am an Orangeman." Two years later, he told the Commons he was an Orangeman first and a politician and M.P. afterwards. "All I boast is that we are a Protestant Parliament and a Protestant state." On 12 July 1933, Sir Basil Brooke, then Minister of Agriculture and later to become Prime Minister, told a meeting in Newtownbutler: "Many in the audience employ Catholics, but I have not one about my place. Catholics are out to destroy Ulster with all their might and power." As tension rose in 1935, Dawson Bates, the Minister of Home Affairs, banned parades and demonstrations—then withdrew the ban after objections by the Orange Order. A dozen people lost their lives in the riots which followed. The city coroner commented: "There would be less bigotry if there was less public speech-making of a kind by so-called leaders of public opinion." The Government refused to hold an official inquiry.

The outbreak of war in 1939 emphasised the differences between the two parts of Ireland. There was no conscription in the North, but the South—which had declared itself a "sovereign, independent, democratic state" in 1937—remained neutral. In addition, the so-called treaty ports which Britain had retained as naval bases since 1921 had been handed over in 1938. Derry became a major base, and Northerners were critical that the South's refusal to enter the war had cost Allied lives in the Atlantic. The war brought employment, and eased some of the religious animosity; the shared experience of bombing raids drew Belfast people together. After the war, the development of the British welfare state—adopted locally in a "step-by-step" policy —emphasised the difference in living standards between Northern Ireland and what became in 1948 the Republic of Ireland, no longer a member of the British Commonwealth. Many Southerners had worked in the North during the war, but the 1947 Safeguarding of Employment Act introduced employment permits and compelled them to leave again. In 1949, the Ireland Act gave Stormont a guarantee on the maintenance of the constitutional position; a general election in February amounted virtually to a referendum on the partition question, with passions roused by the "chapel-gate collections" organised in Dublin to raise funds to fight the Unionists. The Northern Ireland Labour Party lost all its seats at Stormont at this time, and did not return until 1958.

In December 1956, the I.R.A. launched an intensive campaign of violence in Northern Ireland. There had been earlier incidents, including raids on army barracks in Armagh and Omagh in 1954, and an attack on a police station in Roslea, Co. Fermanagh, in which a raider was fatally wounded, in 1955. But now there was a sustained onslaught on symbols of the "British occupation", including army and territorial army barracks, customs posts, even B.B.C. installations. Gradually the attack widened to include bridges, police stations, and public services. In all, there were about 300 major incidents, and six members of the R.U.C. lost their lives; one died leaving a girl friend across the border at Roslea, another in an ambush at Jonesborough, Co. Armagh, another when a booby-trap exploded in a disused farmhouse.

Not all the incidents were the work of the I.R.A., for there were also breakaway Republican groups. During the campaign, which varied in intensity and lasted until February 1962, the Government took additional powers under the Special Powers Act, and at one time close to 200 men were interned. Both the Army and the B Specials were active in defence of Northern Ireland during this period, and the Southern Government also took steps to curb I.R.A. activities. In the 1955 British general election, Sinn Fein contested the 12 Ulster seats and won both Mid-Ulster and Fermanagh–South Tyrone; the successful candidates were convicted felons who had been captured after the Omagh arms raid, and were disqualified and unseated by the courts. In subsequent elections, Republican candidates were unable to command the full Catholic vote, and the seats were both held by Unionists until Bernadette Devlin won Mid-Ulster in 1969. The Sinn Fein successes in 1955 seemed to reflect traditional anti-Unionism, and there was little other evidence that the Catholic population was sympathetic to the I.R.A. This was one reason why no sectarian strife was caused.

Lord Craigavon, as Craig had become, died in 1940. John Andrews held the premiership for a short period before Sir Basil Brooke led a successful revolt in 1943, arguing that the war effort was not being pursued purposefully enough. In May 1962, Lord Brookeborough (as he now was) was still capable of fighting a successful election campaign, but there was a lack of dynamism in his administration. In October, the Government published the report of a joint working party of civil servants from Stormont and Whitehall, under the chairmanship of Sir Robert Hall, on Ulster's economy. It was a gloomy document, and Brookeborough had no new initiative to offer.

It was at this point that Terence O'Neill reinforced his claims to the Premiership with a speech in the Pottinger constituency of Belfast calling for self-help. "We must proceed with a three-pronged attack on our problems, relying largely on our own skill, determination and enterprise." O'Neill had held the senior ministry, Finance, since 1956—his direct experience of the need for the Treasury's goodwill conditioned his political attitudes to an appreciable extent—but had not established his right to succeed Brookeborough. But his Pottinger speech was well received, and he continued to talk in this vein during a winter of high unemployment in which Brookeborough's health and political touch were clearly failing. When the time came for the Chief Whip, William Craig, to take soundings in the party O'Neill appeared to command majority support.

O'Neill and Brookeborough had similar backgrounds. O'Neill's father was the first Westminster M.P. killed in World War one, and two brothers were killed in World War Two; he himself was wounded while serving in the Irish Guards. He had originally hoped for a Westminster seat, but was chosen for Bannside in 1946. The larger world of Westminster might have suited him better, for his view of politics was not parochial; as Finance Minister, he persuaded the Chancellor of the Exchequer that he should be in the British delegation to the World Bank. In his first major speech as Prime Minister, O'Neill told Unionists that the challenge was "literally to transform the face of Ulster". Sir Robert Matthew, the architect, had provided in 1962 a physical plan for the Belfast region, and O'Neill commissioned an economic plan from an Ulster-born economist, Professor Tom Wilson of Glasgow University.

O'Neill's first real break with the past was to settle a long-standing difference between the Government and the trade union movement. The Irish Congress of Trade Unions was based in Dublin, but negotiations led to a degree of autonomy for the I.C.T.U.'s Northern committee which made it politically possible for the Government to recognise it. This allowed an Economic Council to be formed, and trade union leaders began to have much closer contacts with Stormont. Brian Faulkner had become Minister of Commerce and the new industries drive was making a substantial contribution to the economy; the province was still vulnerable to fluctuations in the British economy, but there was certainly new hope and confidence in the business community.

O'Neill also spoke of "building bridges in the community". There had been some abortive talks between the leaders of the Orange and Hibernian orders; O'Neill began the forbidding task of changing people's attitudes, in the belief that the new Ulster he envisaged could not emerge if one-third of the population were reluctant partners removed from the mainstream of Ulster life. But, just as he awakened hopes, so he was criticised for not moving quickly enough. A published correspondence with two Catholic laymen, J. J. Campbell (later on the Cameron Commission) and Brian McGuigan, indicated disappointment that O'Neill was not making more effort to ensure that Catholics were appointed to public bodies. The Prime Minister often found himself in the difficult position of having to guard against criticism from his own right-wing, and consequently defending the slow rate of progress in terms which alienated those whose participation he wanted to encourage. At the same time, he did undertake one bold move which seemed to introduce a completely new era in Irish politics. This was his invitation to the Southern Premier, Sean Lemass, to visit Stormont. The meeting was arranged through Kenneth Whitaker, the Ulster-born secretary of the Republic's Department of Finance, whom O'Neill had got to know at World Bank meetings.

On Thursday, 14 January 1965, Sean Lemass drove through

the gates of Stormont. It was a well-kept secret, so much so that O'Neill's Cabinet colleagues had not been told in advance; nor had leading Unionist officials or the Orange Order. "Things can never be the same again so far as North–South relations are concerned," Lemass commented afterwards. For O'Neill, too, things were never the same. It was a dramatic and triumphant gesture, and—as in the 1969 general election—was an appeal to public opinion over the heads of diehard supporters who were unwilling to countenance change. He emphasised that the talks had centred on economic matters, and that there had been no question of discussing political or constitutional issues. In a general election in November, aided by cold weather which curbed Labour's vote in the final hours of polling, O'Neill scored a personal success. But he had aroused implacable enmity in some quarters, and had forfeited the trust of close colleagues because he had not trusted them.

The handling of the meeting with Lemass was typical of O'Neill's style of government. On gaining power, he had altered the balance of politics. Billy Douglas, Unionist secretary for many years and a masterly politician of the Tammany Hall school, quickly retired. There was soon a new head of the Civil Service, and a new secretary to the Cabinet; O'Neill's advisers were a close-knit group of civil servants, a kitchen cabinet sometimes described as the presidential aides. The Cabinet was never a united team—O'Neill was conscious of Faulkner's rivalry, though he tried to assuage this by making Faulkner Deputy Premier—and there was poor contact with the constituencies. Brookeborough, a practical farmer and former Minister of Agriculture, had a common touch which always eluded his successor. O'Neill was never at home in Orange halls as Faulkner was; he was an indifferent performer in Parliament, and made many of his best speeches on non-political occasions where he was more sure of a welcome for progressive ideas. His vision was never matched by a capacity to carry people along with him, and his gains seemed to be eroded away by men more dogmatic and fanatical than he was. Outside the party, the most persistent of his critics was Ian Paisley.

Paisley had been around for a good many years, a demagogue in a familiar Ulster clerical tradition. His father was a Baptist pastor in Ballymena, Co. Antrim, who set up his own gospel tabernacle following a dispute within his church. Paisley attended the training college of the Reformed Presbyterian Church in Belfast, then studied at the Barrie School of Evangelism in Wales. His degrees have come from evangelical institutions in the United States, of which the best known is probably Bob Jones University in South Carolina. Towards the end of the war, he preached at Ravenhill Evangelical Mission Church in Belfast; its congregation had split away from orthodox Presbyterianism, and Paisley subsequently received a call to the church. This was the foundation of the Free Presbyterian Church, which has grown partly by exploiting other local disputes.

Often he made headlines. In 1956, a 15-year-old Catholic girl called Maura Lyons disappeared. She had attended a number of Paisley's meetings, and at one point Paisley played in the Ulster Hall a tape-recording (supposedly of the missing girl) in which a girl's voice told of escaping from a "religion of fear and dread". Maura Lyons turned up at Paisley's house on her sixteenth birthday, and was later made a ward of court and returned to her family. Visiting clerics like Donald Soper and Leslie Weatherhead were assailed by Paisley and his followers. At one time, Paisley was closely associated with an organisation called Ulster Protestant Action, whose purpose was "to permeate all activities, social and cultural, with Protestant ideals, and in the accomplishment of this end it is primarily dedicated to immediate action in the sphere of employment". More than once, he has demonstrated in Rome against Protestant clergy visiting the Vatican.

O'Neill's first real experience of Paisley's power came during the Westminster general election of 1964. A tricolour had been displayed in the window of the Republican Party's Divis Street headquarters. Paisley announced a protest march, but this was banned by the Minister of Home Affairs, Brian McConnell; police then broke down the door of the headquarters on Monday, 28 September and removed the tricolour. The Republican candidate, Liam McMillan, announced that another tricolour would be put up if the police did not return the one they had taken. On Wednesday afternoon, the police removed the second flag. The jeers and chanting which greeted the two police raids gradually turned into violence, as youths from different parts of the city gathered in search of trouble. Not until the weekend did peace return, by which time the police had been attacked by bricks, bottles and petrol bombs. O'Neill's criticism of Paisley's contribution was oblique: "While I can understand the provocation which exists where men associated with the I.R.A. offer themselves as candidates for a parliament in which they do not intend to sit, equally no one can condone any utterance or action which, wittingly or unwittingly, contributes to a breach of the peace."

Paisley's challenge intensified in 1966. The world-wide ecumenical movement had aroused Protestant fears in Northern Ireland, and the ground was made more fertile for Paisley's anti-Catholicism by the fact that special celebrations were planned to mark the 50th anniversary of the 1916 Easter rising in Dublin. The first controversy was over the naming of a new bridge over the River Lagan in Belfast, which was to be opened by Queen Elizabeth. Right-wing Unionists on the city council wanted to name it Carson Bridge, but many people argued for a less divisive name; eventually, a message from the recently appointed Governor, Lord Erskine, led to the bridge being named after the Queen herself. Soon afterwards, a letter from Carson's son Edward, a former Conservative M.P., asked: "Why should Her Majesty be embarrassed by the use of my father's name? He was one of the most loyal subjects that have ever served the Crown, and was treated with scant veneration by successive Governments in the Imperial Parliament. . . ." Carson was taken up by Paisley, and efforts were made to manœuvre Unionist headquarters into finding a seat for him at the approaching Westminster election. But these efforts failed, and Carson—who seemed politically naïve, and embarrassed his supporters by advocating that Ulster's public houses should open on Sundays—withdrew a threat to stand against the official candidate in North Belfast, where his father's seat had been.

The election on 31 March gave Gerry Fitt victory over the sitting Unionist in West Belfast. This broke the Unionist monopoly of the 12 Ulster seats, and Fitt proved a skilled publicist, awakening a good deal of Labour backbench interest in the grievances of the Catholic minority in Northern Ireland. The Easter rising celebrations followed almost immediately, on successive weekends, and Paisley threatened to hold rival parades. On 8 April, O'Neill made a brave speech at a joint Protestant–Catholic conference at Corrymeela, Co. Antrim, almost on the eve of the first parades. He said the Government would stand up to noisy minorities, whatever section of the community they might come from, and called on people to "shed the burdens of traditional grievances and ancient resentments". He noted that many people had questioned "whether the maintenance of two distinct educational systems side by side is not wasteful of human and financial resources, and a major barrier to the promotion of communal understanding". This soon drew a rebuke from Cardinal Conway.

In December, Brian McConnell had announced that the Government had received information indicating that the I.R.A. were planning to renew subversive activities directed against Northern Ireland. The Government's security committee, dormant since the earlier I.R.A. campaign, was reactivated; its members were O'Neill, McConnell, and other Cabinet Ministers who had previously held Home Affairs. As Easter Sunday, 10 April, approached, the Government outlined to the public the measures it had taken to guard against new violence and said: "The creation of communal disorder would, of course, not only besmirch the good name of Ulster but also play into the hands of the I.R.A., who would clearly welcome the opportunity of exploiting such a situation."

The Government in Dublin was also apprehensive—and with good reason, for early on the morning of 8 April a familiar Dublin landmark, Nelson's Pillar, was demolished by an explosion. The North had experienced a number of minor incidents, including petrol bomb attacks on Catholic schools and on a police Land Rover. A dozen Republican parades were planned for Easter Sunday, and McConnell banned one of them—at Loup, Co. Derry—on the grounds that it would undoubtedly have led to serious public disorder. The Ulster Constitution Defence Committee cancelled rival parades that it had planned for different parts of Northern Ireland. The following Sunday, there was a threat of rival parades clashing in Belfast, where the celebrations were concentrated, but there was no major incident. McConnell made an order banning rail travel from Dublin to Belfast from Saturday night to Sunday night, and there was close scrutiny of road traffic crossing the border. There were a number of prosecutions arising from failure to give formal notice of parades.

On the evening of Monday, 6 June, Paisley led a march from his church to protest against "Romanising tendencies" in the Presbyterian General Assembly. The route passed through Belfast's markets area, a Catholic stronghold, and Paisley had pointed out publicly that no Protestant parade had passed that way since before the war. The provocation found a ready response, and more than 200 Catholics were waiting to throw bricks, nuts and bolts, bottles and other missiles. The attack on the march only lasted a few minutes, but there were sporadic battles with the police for several more hours. Meanwhile Paisley and his followers had reached the Assembly Buildings, where they marched round the block. The Assembly's guests included Lord and Lady Erskine, who were jeered at as they crossed the street. Lady Erskine was so distressed by the experience that she had to receive medical attention at Government House, and her ill health eventually led Erskine to resign in 1968.

Both O'Neill and McConnell were in London for talks at the Home Office. They immediately returned, and O'Neill told the Commons that "the organisers of any such demonstration will be required in the future to establish beyond doubt that what they propose is not likely to lead to disorder in the city". McConnell denied a suggestion that he had overruled the police when they wanted to re-route the march; the police had considered a breach of the peace unlikely. He then visited the General Assembly, and made an abject apology for the disturbances, promising that "the Government will take all possible steps to prevent a recurrence of such indignities to the head of our great Church and his distinguished guests". The Moderator was Dr Alfred Martin, whose year of office was notable for his outspoken criticism of extremism. He replied briefly: "We accept the expression of regret which you have brought. We have asked you for a written assurance that such happening as took place on Monday night will not occur again. When we receive this, it will be recorded in our minutes." Paisley, for his part, said it was evident that O'Neill was prepared to use the police to "quell mounting opposition to his treacherous policies". and warned that "as Protestants we are as determined as the gun-runners of Larne not to bow to tyranny from any source".

On Tuesday, 19 July, Paisley was found guilty of unlawful assembly on 6 June. He and four other men were each fined £30 and ordered to enter into a rule of bail of £30 to keep the peace and be of good behaviour for two years. A woman was fined £5 and ordered to enter into rule of bail. Paisley and two others—both Free Presbyterian clergymen—chose to go to prison for three months. During the week, there were disturbances outside the Crumlin Road prison, and on Friday night shops were looted in nearby Old Lodge Road after police had used batons and water cannon. A Free Presbyterian parade to the City Hall was planned for Saturday afternoon, but police made an order confining it to the Shankill Road area. Again police had to use batons and water cannon as some marchers tried to force their way past a police cordon. A few demonstrators eventually reached the city centre and smashed some windows. On 26 July, McConnell made an order banning for three months public processions or meetings, other than traditional ones, within a 15-mile radius of the City Hall.

Meanwhile, on 28 June, O'Neill had announced that the Minister of Home Affairs had made an order under the Special Powers Act declaring the Ulster Volunteer Force an illegal organisation. Not much was known about the U.V.F., but in May newspaper offices in Belfast had received by telephone a statement allegedly from Captain William Johnston, adjutant of the 1st Belfast battalion. It said: "From this day we declare war against the I.R.A. and its splinter groups. Known I.R.A. men will be executed mercilessly and without hesitation." On 27 May, a 28-year-old Catholic called John Patrick Scullion was taken to hospital in Belfast with wounds from which he died on 11 June. He was said to have died of a stab wound, but anonymous telephone calls to newspapers suggested he had been shot by the U.V.F. and his body was later exhumed. Then, in the early hours of Sunday, 26 June, a young Catholic barman, called Peter Ward, emerged with three friends from a public house in Malvern Street where they had been drinking after hours. They were met with a hail of bullets; 18-year-old Ward was dead on arrival in hospital, and two others were injured. Not long afterwards, a 77-year-old Protestant widow, Matilda Gould, died from injuries she had received when a petrol bomb was thrown into her home in Upper Charleville Street in May. She had lived beside a Catholic-owned public house, and it was assumed that the bomb had missed its target; there were attacks on other Catholic premises the same weekend.

Within a few hours of Ward's death, the police had arrested three men—Augustus "Gusty" Spence, Hugh Arnold McLean and Robert John Williamson—and in October they were finally found guilty of murder. They were found not guilty on a capital charge of committing murder in the course or furtherance of a seditious conspiracy or of activities associated with an unlawful organisation; none the less, the Lord Chief Justice, Lord MacDermott, sentenced them to life with a minimum of 20 years in prison. In passing sentence, he said it was abun-

dantly clear that some sort of conspiracy might have been at
the bottom of the killing. One written statement, alleged to
have been made by McLean, described how he joined the
Shankill Road division of the U.V.F. under Spence. Evidence
was also given that, when charged, McLean said: "I am sorry
I ever heard tell of that man Paisley or decided to follow him."
Spence was charged with Scullion's murder also, but the
Crown dropped the case against him.

A number of other men were jailed in 1966. One of them was
26-year-old Noel Doherty, described as former secretary of the
Ulster Constitution Defence Committee and a director of the
company which printed Paisley's *Protestant Telegraph*. He
received a two-year sentence when he pleaded guilty to conspiring to provide explosives to persons unknown for the
purpose of endangering life or causing serious injury to property.
Another man, James Burns, was jailed for nine years; Lord
MacDermott said he had "either graduated or was in the
course of graduating to become a gunman". Three men got
sentences of four years each, arising from a shooting incident
at Crimea Street on 16 June, following a Paisley parade to the
Ulster Hall.

Paisley himself was quick to disclaim any association with
the Ulster Volunteer Force. Shortly after the U.V.F. was
declared illegal, he told a meeting in Holywood, Co. Down,
that he had no knowledge of its activities. "As a Christian and
as a Protestant minister, I deplore and condemn anyone who
would dare to take the law into their own hands and shoot
down their fellows, no matter what their colour, class or creed."
On 29 June, O'Neill told the Commons: "He is no doubt
anxious to wash his hands of them now. But the record clearly
shows that he has hitherto received and welcomed their
support." O'Neill referred to a verbatim report of Paisley's
Ulster Hall speech on 16 June, when he welcomed a resolution
of support from four divisions of the U.V.F. He referred also to
an Ulster Hall meeting on 17 April, when Paisley had thanked
members of the U.V.F. for marching with him that day.
O'Neill also revealed that the police had informed him that a

leading member of the U.V.F. was also an important official of the Ulster Constitution Defence Committee. Paisley later claimed he had been quoted out of context, and there was no reply when he challenged O'Neill to name the official.

Queen Elizabeth's visit to Northern Ireland had been arranged for July, and there was some debate about whether it was safe for her to come. There were two incidents on 4 July, shortly after the Queen had opened the new bridge. An Englishwoman, with a disturbed mental background, threw a bottle as the royal procession passed. A Catholic youth threw a concrete block, denting the bonnet of the royal car, from a building under construction—as "a personal protest".

O'Neill soon ran into his first major leadership crisis, as right-wing M.P.s circulated a petition claiming he had failed to unite the people and the party behind him in his policies. On Friday, 23 September, O'Neill issued a sharply worded statement: "On returning from a very brief holiday, during which I carried out several official engagements, I find that a conspiracy has been mounted against me in my absence. I have only this to say—I will fight this out; I believe that my policies represent the best safeguard to our constitutional position and our best hope for prosperity."

Brian Faulkner quickly issued a statement saying that there was a feeling of discontent in the party, and that he had advised the Chief Whip, James Chichester-Clark, of what he knew. It was thought that three members of the Cabinet would have welcomed a change of leadership: Faulkner, Harry West, the Minister of Agriculture, and William Morgan, Minister of Health and Social Services.

The Unionist Parliamentary Party met on Tuesday, 27 September, by which time it was evident that the revolt was collapsing. Faulkner had left for an industrial promotion visit to America at the weekend, and 27 out of 29 M.P.s present supported a motion of confidence which was then made unanimous. A similar motion was passed by Senators with one abstention. The meeting lasted almost seven hours, and covered the Lemass meetings, the Easter rising celebrations,

Paisleyism and local sources of discontent like the closing of railways in the western counties and compulsory land purchases in the new city of Craigavon. In part, the revolt was caused by O'Neill's aloof style of government, and the backbenchers decided to set up a 66 Committee on the lines of the Conservative 1922 Committee at Westminster. Early in October, O'Neill reshuffled his Government, with Craig moving from Development (railways and the new city, which he had named amid controversy, were among his responsibilities) into Home Affairs in place of McConnell.

During the difficult summer, when Ulster's troubles were featured in newspapers and on television screens throughout the world, the British Government took a new interest in Northern Ireland. On 5 August, O'Neill had "frank and friendly" talks with Harold Wilson and the Home Secretary, Roy Jenkins, at Downing Street. Economic issues were also discussed; Belfast's shipyard and aircraft factory were causing some concern, and a financial squeeze threatened unemployment which could jeopardise O'Neills long-term hopes.

A few days later, Alice Bacon, Minister of State at the Home Office, made an important statement on Britain's responsibility for Northern Ireland. She said that in no event could there be any question of the British Government interfering in matters transferred to Stormont without legislation passed by virtue of Section 75 of the Government of Ireland Act. She said this section preserved the supreme authority of the United Kingdom Parliament, but not of the British Government, over transferred matters. Wilson, she said, did not favour intervention under Section 75, or the setting up of an inquiry into the working of the 1920 Act. He preferred the method of informal talks.

There was another Downing Street meeting on 12 January 1967, when it appeared that Wilson was satisfied with the momentum of change undertaken by the Northern Ireland Government. The Government had by then announced its intention to abolish the business vote in Stormont elections, and to abolish and redistribute the four Queen's University seats; a boundary commission was to delineate the new seats in the Belfast area, where housing developments had created oversized constituencies, and then to spend more time over recommendations for the whole province.

Craig, who attended the Downing Street meeting in January, warned in March that Westminster interference would be resisted, and said that "Ulster will fight and Ulster will be right . . . this sort of attack and interference would mobilise Ulster loyalists in the same way as attacks by bomb and bullet."

Paisley continued his criticism of O'Neill when he emerged from prison, but his next major victory was the cancellation of a lecture by the Bishop of Ripon, Dr John Moorman. Moorman had led the Anglican delegation in talks with Catholic theologians at Gazzada, in Italy, in January. The Irish Church Association, a small group of clergy and laymen who held lunch-time meetings to hear talks about modern trends in the Church, invited him to speak in Belfast on Monday, 6 February. Because so many people asked for tickets, it was arranged to hold the lecture in St Anne's Cathedral, in Belfast, and to have the bishop preach there on the preceding Sunday.

Moorman had expressed the view that, if there were ever a united Christian Church, it would seem natural that the Pope— as head of the largest denomination—should preside. Paisley announced that he would protest, and he was joined in his condemnation of the visit by the County Grand Orange Lodge of Belfast. On Monday, 30 January, the Dean of Belfast— Cuthbert Peacocke, brother of the man who was to become Inspector-General of the R.U.C.—withdrew both permission for the meeting and the invitation to preach. He revealed he had consulted the Government. Moorman then cancelled his visit altogether.

Easter again posed problems, for it was the centenary of the 1867 Fenian rising, and on 7 March Craig announced a complete ban on all processions specifically linked to this. However, there was provision for traditional Easter celebrations, provided they were so organised as to minimise and contain "the offence given to the majority of citizens", and provided specific permission was obtained from the R.U.C. The Ancient Order of Hibernians immediately cancelled traditional St Patrick's Day demonstrations rather than apply for permission, but Coleraine members decided to defy the ban by marching in Maghera. Police in Belfast then granted permission, without being asked, for the traditional Easter Sunday parade to Milltown cemetery. Paisley called off an Easter Sunday parade planned by the Ulster Constitution Defence Committee.

On 7 March, Craig also announced that he had made an order under the Special Powers Act proscribing Republican clubs. He said there were some 40 clubs in Northern Ireland, a substantial proportion of whose members were connected with the I.R.A. or Sinn Fein. He said he had received a detailed report from the Inspector-General, from which it emerged that "the organisation is substantially the unlawful Sinn Fein organisation under another label". Craig's move was widely interpreted as an attempt to appease extreme Protestants—a counter-balance to the other ban, which would prevent them staging counter-demonstrations.

On Sunday, 19 March, the Northern directorate of Republican clubs called a meeting in Belfast to protest against the ban, and police took a number of men into custody for questioning. The most significant outcome of the ban was probably the formation of a Republican club at Queen's University. The club was approved by the students' representative council in May, but in November the Academic Council formally refused to recognise it. The students then announced that they would march to Unionist headquarters in Belfast on 15 November to protest against the ban. This was met by a call for a rally of trade union loyalists, and Paisley complained that the students would go through a Protestant area "for the sole purpose of inciting Protestants".

On 15 November, Paisley held an open-air meeting in Shaftesbury Square, and later held a second meeting at the City Hall. The students were re-routed to Craig's house, where the permanent secretary in Home Affairs was given a letter demanding that the ban be revoked. Craig later suggested the club should change its name, but the students refused. On the whole, the ban proved ineffectual, but it had the effect of stirring up student opposition to the Unionist administration and to Craig himself, and this was to prove an important factor when the civil rights campaign got under way.

O'Neill was faced with another leadership crisis in April 1967, when he dismissed Harry West from the Government. Some years before, O'Neill had laid down a code of conduct for Ministers in situations where there was a possible conflict between private interests and public duties, and he considered West had breached this. It was a complicated issue, involving the price West was to receive from Fermanagh county council for land which was to be used as an airport; West had earlier bought the land from a cousin who had fallen on hard times. There was no suggestion of dishonesty, but West later spoke of his "solemn conviction that a deliberate attempt had been made to discredit me in the House and in the eyes of the public".

In a community whose roots were largely rural, West's attachment to family land seemed understandable, and there was a good deal of sympathy for him; the executive committee of Fermanagh Unionist Association immediately passed a vote of no confidence in the Premier. Brian Faulkner commented that the former Minister of Agriculture was "certainly absolutely blameless", and there was speculation that he might resign. However, he subsequently declared that under no consideration would he allow his name to be linked "at this time" with any attempt to usurp the leadership of the party. After West had made a personal statement to the Commons, the 66 Committee met and supported the Premier's action. When Chichester-Clark suggested on television that Faulkner should give an unreserved and unequivocal declaration of support for the Premier, the Minister of Commerce commented: "All that is left is to pledge to support Capt. O'Neill on every issue that will ever arise in this country, right or wrong. That pledge I would not give to the Archangel Gabriel himself were he to become Prime Minister."

By the end of the year, O'Neill felt secure enough to invite to Stormont Jack Lynch, who had succeeded Lemass in November 1966. There had been a number of unpromising verbal exchanges during the year—as there had been in the months before the Lemass visit—but on 11 December 1967 Lynch arrived at Stormont. On 8 January O'Neill returned the visit, and discussions ranged from foot-and-mouth precautions to cultural exchanges. Soon afterwards, the Ulster Museum was able to exhibit on loan the Killymoon gold hoard, a collection of bronze age bracelets from Co. Tyrone; in November, it had been outbid by the Republic's National Museum when the collection was auctioned in London.

For the third year in succession, Easter raised the political temperature. The Ulster Protestant Volunteers announced an Easter Sunday march in Armagh, where there was also to be a traditional parade commemorating 1916. Captain Long, acting Minister of Home Affairs in Craig's temporary absence, banned both because he was convinced that "the processions in this area would lead to serious public disorder". The traditional parade was held, in spite of a police warning that it was banned, and six of the organisers were eventually fined.

In February, O'Neill had addressed a meeting of the Irish Association for Cultural, Economic and Social Relations in Belfast. It was his first major speech on community relations since Corrymeela, two years before, and he spoke of "an occupation of a broad area of middle ground by reasonable men and its steady widening in course of time." But O'Neill had to deal with too many unreasonable men, and he wrote his own epitaph in the same speech when he said: "In fact, the power of a Prime Minister is virtually synonymous with his influence—with his ability to put across and gain general support for some consistent body of opinions and policies. Action by words is an essential forerunner in difficult and contentious matters to action by deeds. And in many respects it is the only possible form of action." O'Neill had aroused hopes that he had been unable to fulfil, and Northern Ireland was soon to pay the price.

5. The Dividing Line

Belfast's ghettoes, scarred by violence since August 1969, are possibly the most dramatic evidence of the cleavage between Protestants and Catholics in Northern Ireland. But the division runs through the whole community, and even where it is bridged people are usually conscious that it is being bridged—and perhaps that they are making a deliberate effort to bridge it. Is it essentially a religious division? Or is it political in origin? Is it perhaps a social division, the product of centuries of segregation? Is it the difference between settler and native, a difference which might be more readily recognised if the Catholics had dark skins? Is there an analogy with the Southern states of America, with the Catholics cast as negroes, the Shankill Road Protestants as poor whites needing an inferior group to boost their own self-esteem? Do Ulster's Tories continue to play the Orange card, so that their ascendancy is not challenged by a united working class?

Certainly, there is a political division. The majority of Protestants have traditionally supported the Unionist Party, while the Catholics have voted Nationalist. The socialist cause has never flourished, and has proved very vulnerable when—as in 1949—the border issue loomed large in an election campaign. The Northern Ireland Labour Party was forced to take a pro-constitution stand at that time, and the Republican Labour Party has increasingly taken command of the Catholic urban ghettoes in Belfast. The Nationalist Party is predominantly a rural party, and in some areas the National Democratic Party has emerged to give expression to a recent desire (particularly among middle-class Catholics) to play a more constructive role. The Liberals are less successful than their cross-channel counterparts, and lost their only seat at Stormont when the four Queen's University seats were abolished in 1969.

The political situation is not wholly inflexible; in 1969, the Nationalists lost three of their nine seats to Independents closely associated with the civil rights campaign, while three Independent pro-O'Neill Unionists won seats. But there is a safe Unionist majority at Stormont, reflecting the importance Protestants attach to the constitutional issue, and it seems unassailable except by the emergence of a breakaway party which—while fostering closer relations between Protestants and Catholics—would unequivocally support the British link.

It is a fact of Ulster politics that the two most successful parties, in terms of their electoral record through the years, are the two which are almost totally sectarian in membership. The membership of the Labour and Liberal parties is much more mixed, and so is their support; but they have not done well at the polls, and they find voters fickle. The Labour Party did recover slowly from the 1949 debacle, when it lost all representation in the Commons at Stormont, but O'Neill successfully turned a rising tide by putting more emphasis on economic issues when he fought the 1965 election. Moreover, Northern Ireland's economy is very much influenced by national policy, and it is arguable that the real economic choice in Northern Ireland is not between conservative Unionism and socialism but between Great Britain and the Republic of Ireland.

The Nationalist Party has always been rather loosely organised, and only in recent years has it made much attempt to provide a coherent Opposition. In the 1960s it began to feel some pressure from a new body called National Unity, composed of middle-class Catholics in business and the professions who wanted a more positive role in Ulster life. Attempts to unite the different anti-partition groups came to nothing, but the National Democratic Party was born out of this more forward-looking spirit. The Nationalists remained secure in their Catholic strongholds, or so it seemed until the civil rights movement turned the Catholic population's attention to objectives more attainable than a united Ireland. In the early days of Northern Ireland, Nationalists abstained from Parliament, and when they have attended it has usually been as the voice of an oppressed minority. They did, of course, prove vulnerable in the 1950s to the Sinn Fein Party, which fought all 12 Westminster seats (and won two, only to have the successful candidates disqualified because they were serving jail sentences in connection with I.R.A. raids). If the Nationalists have disappointed, it must be said that they have had no encouragement from the Unionists to provide constructive Opposition; nor have they had the prospect of a change in government to sustain them.

The Unionists dominate Ulster politics. The party is essentially a conservative one, though it embraces the whole social spectrum of Protestants; its Westminster members accept the Conservative whip. The original link with the Orange Order has been preserved, and membership of the order has usually been a prerequisite to a political career. It must be said, though, that in the autumn of 1969 three members of the Cabinet were not in the Orange Order; Phelim O'Neill (Agriculture) had been expelled, William Fitzsimmons (Health and Social Services) had resigned when his daughter married a Catholic, and Dr Robert Simpson resigned from the Orange and Masonic Orders on being appointed to the new post of Minister of Community Relations. On the other hand, Richard Ferguson, one of the liberal group of Unionist M.P.s, received a vote of no confidence from his constituency association in September 1969 when he resigned from the Orange Order, saying "Now is the time for all people in Northern Ireland to try to come together."

In 1959, in answer to a question at a Young Unionist political school at Portstewart, the then chairman of the party's standing committee said he did not see why a Catholic should not be chosen as a Unionist parliamentary candidate. The ensuing controversy lasted several weeks, and Sir George Clark, then

Grand Master of the Grand Orange Lodge of Ireland, said that the order would not countenance Catholics joining the party. In practice, a decision on whether or not to admit Catholics to membership rests with local associations. The link with the Orange Order obviously deters many Catholics from applying.

The *raison d'être* of Unionism is the maintenance of the union with Great Britain, but in fact the Unionist position has changed substantially over the years. The fact that Ulster Unionists organised themselves separately indicated that they were prepared to concentrate on one part of the island, and to abandon Southern Unionists when the time came. Additionally, they agreed to abandon the Unionists in three of the nine Ulster counties, so that the Protestant majority would be more assured in the six which remained British. They had no desire to have a separate Parliament, but it was soon realised that it provided an instrument for maintaining the Protestant ascendancy and for resisting any attempt to coerce the North into a united Ireland. While the subordinate Parliament existed, it was unlikely that Westminster would countenance a united Ireland without its approval. In 1949, the Ireland Act put this on a more formal basis with a specific assurance.

For a number of years, Unionist Party headquarters in Belfast bore a large sign proclaiming "Ulster is British". But what did being British mean? The Unionist Government had developed a step-by-step policy, by which it copied Westminster legislation in a number of fields and most closely in the developing social services and benefits of the welfare state. But in a number of areas the Unionists were slow to adopt British reforms. The local government franchise was the most widely publicised issue in the civil rights campaign, but there were others such as legal aid and compensation for victims of criminal violence.

In 1956, it was proposed to deviate from the British pattern of family allowances in a way that would have benefited smaller families as against larger ones; this was abandoned in the face of opposition in Northern Ireland and in Great

Britain, for it was clear that the objective was to reduce the benefits to Catholics. A British scheme to relieve ratepayers on low incomes was amended so that the relief went directly to local authorities, and the major beneficiaries were the larger ratepayers. There was resistance to establishing an ombudsman and to introducing a local equivalent of the Race Relations Act. The Unionists were always ready to make great use of the symbols of Britishness—the national anthem is almost a party song, the Union Jack is widely used in election posters—but their critics accused them of not adhering to the spirit of British parliamentary democracy. It was not hard to see parallels with the situation in Rhodesia, where white settlers protested their loyalty to the Crown while resisting reforms which might have undermined their position.

There are grounds for thinking that the Protestant population as a whole were significantly more liberal in outlook than the Unionist Party, whose leaders were always conscious of the deep conservatism of the party faithfuls. There seemed a strong popular welcome for the Lemass–O'Neill meetings in 1965, and Captain O'Neill won a handsome election victory later in the year. In 1967, the *Belfast Telegraph* commissioned National Opinion Polls Limited to carry out an independent survey of public opinion in Northern Ireland, and the results were encouraging to liberal opinion. There were substantial proportions of the electorate in favour of the Government trying to improve relations with the Republic (74 per cent), in favour of greater efforts to promote Christian unity (82 per cent), in favour of Protestants and Catholics trying to get on better with each other (96 per cent thought this was important). The figures for Unionist voters naturally reflected Protestant doubts—Catholics generally took more liberal attitudes—but there was no hint of massive resistance to change.

Perhaps the most interesting question asked which of three constitutional arrangements would be best for Ireland. A total of 42 per cent approved the existing situation, 12 per cent preferred the traditional Nationalist objective of a united and independent Ireland, and a surprising 44 per cent opted for a united Ireland linked with Great Britain. The nature of the link was not specified, but the figures certainly hinted at a body of opinion which would countenance constitutional change in the hope of reaching a final solution to the Irish question. About half the electorate thought the border would eventually disappear, and about one-third that it would go within 25 years.

But Unionist spokesmen were inclined to point out that a total of 86 per cent of the electorate favoured a link with Britain, and certainly it is true that few Northern Protestants would wish to be in an independent Irish republic. It is not merely that they are *for* Great Britain—as indicated above, aspects of British life are resisted—but that they are *against* the Republic. It is an indication of fundamental Unionist–Protestant outlooks that the ruling political slogans are negative ones: Not an inch, No surrender, No Pope here. There is an economic advantage in the British link, particularly with subsidies of over £100m. a year flowing out of the British Exchequer. Unionists sometimes accuse Nationalists of being loyal, not to the Crown but to the half-crown, but the jibe can as easily be turned back on the governing party. But, outside economics, there is a deep distrust of Roman Catholicism and the assumed power of the Catholic Church in the Republic. To support partition is a political attitude, but it is rooted deep in religion. The Protestant who practises or approves of discrimination is motivated both by anti-Catholicism and by fear that his Catholic neighbours may eventually get the upper hand. No political party deliberately invites its own destruction or the destruction of the political and constitutional system it supports, so the attitude of such Unionists is at least understandable. But there are certainly grounds for doubting whether a Catholic majority would vote Northern Ireland into the Republic, and O'Neill's view was that fair treatment would ensure that enough supported the Union.

It is probably true that much of the religious bigotry which exists in Northern Ireland stems from ignorance about the other man's religion—and, indeed, many would describe themselves as Protestants without being able to say which Protestant denomination they supported. Church attendances are certainly higher than in England, but for a minority (which might contain a high proportion of trouble-makers) Protestantism might better be defined as anti-Catholicism. Many Protestants feel that their Catholic neighbours look on them as heretics who are destined for eternal damnation, and in turn feel that Catholics are likely to be denied salvation because of their Church's errors. The Catholic Church often appears a monolithic organisation, with tight clerical discipline over the laity—a view which is possibly encouraged by the relative fragmentation of Protestantism, with a myriad of evangelical sects outside the main denominations. Certainly, the Catholic Church in Ireland reflects the years of oppression, and the priest's education has traditionally given him a special place in poor communities.

There are, of course, theological differences. But it is rather at the points where the moral and social outlooks of the Catholic Church touch on Protestant–Catholic relations that Protestants take offence. One source of grievance is the *Ne temere* decree, which obliges the parties to a mixed marriage to be married in a Catholic church, and to give undertakings about the religious upbringing of children. Some Protestants believe that the Catholic Church encourages mixed marriages as a means of diminishing the Protestant population, and point especially to the diminution of the Protestant population of the Republic. But it is probably true that the Churches as a whole discourage mixed marriages, which are obviously subject to more stresses in Northern Ireland than they would be in more tolerant communities.

The Northern Protestant is ready to find fault with life in the Republic, attributing political attitudes and policies to the influence of the Catholic Church without admitting that the Protestant Churches have had a substantial influence in the North (in educational policy, for example, and in licensing laws). Critics point to literary censorship in the Republic, to the bans on divorce and the sale of contraceptives, to the "special position" of the Catholic Church under Article 44 of the 1937 Constitution. The most commonly cited example of clerical interference in politics is the 1950 Mother and Child Bill, which proposed free maternity treatment and free medical attention for children up to the age of sixteen. When the hierarchy objected that the proposed scheme was "in direct opposition to the rights of the family and of the individual and are liable to very great abuse", the Government dropped the Bill and the Minister of Health, Dr Noel Browne, resigned.

There are, too, genuine differences of character between Protestant and Catholic—and the differences are heightened, perhaps, by the things they have in common. They share a sense of history, a peasant feeling for traditional values; the industrial revolution has not uprooted Northerners to any great extent, and urban dwellers often retain their links with rural Ulster. Sectors of Ulster society remain very ingrown, clinging to old hostilities. The Protestant tends to cautious puritanism, constructing his life with a view to the future. The Catholic is a more social animal, living eloquently for the day. But there is a Northern hardness in both groups, and Southern Catholics are not wholly at home with either. The Northern Catholic, though, feels himself to be Irish and the beneficiary of a deep heritage which springs from the land he inhabits. The Protestant has not quite learned to make the best of both worlds, to be both Irish and British, and is still searching for a constructive identity to supplant the insecure siege mentality.

Catholic and Protestant live different, largely segregated lives. On Sunday, the Catholic attends Mass and feels free to play Gaelic football or go dancing. The Protestant hesitates to cut his grass on a Sunday, keeps the cinemas closed, and engages (at council level) in acrimonious debates about whether the swings in children's playgrounds should be chained up on the sabbath. Individual recreations like golf or sailing or driving to the beach have become accepted, but organised sports like football or cricket are out of the question. There is a fear that Ulster will succumb to what is generally called the Continental Sunday.

Many social activities are organised around the church—
the tendency has grown, indeed, as churches have fought to
maintain their place in an increasingly secular society. Sporting
activities reflect the religious division, for Catholic schools
have tended not to play such "foreign" games as rugby and
cricket, though this has far from been the case in the Republic.
Gaelic football, hurling and camogie (kinds of hockey played
respectively by men and women) are almost exclusively
Catholic games, and are encouraged by the Gaelic Athletic
Association as an expression of national spirit. Association
football is played by both Protestants and Catholics, but
matches often provide an occasion for spectators to demon-
strate sectarian feelings. Some sports are organised on an all-
Ireland basis, and some divided between North and South;
political and religious issues do tend to arise from time to
time, but do not often effect a disruption.

There is a good deal of intermixing in the arts, both at a
professional and amateur level, and in movements such as
Rotary and business and professional women's clubs. The
fear of intermarriage deters mixing at youth club level, and
the dance-hall probably provides the major meeting place
for young Protestants and Catholics (though the former are
not likely to be at Sunday dances). Many professional organisations recognise no religious distinctions, though there may
be independent sub-groups confined to Catholics or Protestants.

There is much less discrimination in private employment
than there once was, in part because of labour shortages
(despite continuing unemployment), and in part because small
family firms have tended to give way to larger organisations
controlled from outside Northern Ireland and staffed to some
extent by imported executives who are not interested in
religious differences. But where trade unions have an influence
on recruitment, with son following father, Catholic opportunities will still tend to be limited. Small shopkeepers tend to
choose employees of the same religion, and possibly fear the
commercial consequences of doing otherwise, but it is not
unnatural when there is so much segregation in housing.

Refusal to employ a person of different religion is sometimes
excused by saying that the other workers would make trouble.
Where Catholics are employed, they may find themselves in
the poorer paid jobs, and it is much more common to find a
Protestant supervising Catholics than the reverse situation.
Unemployment has traditionally been heaviest in areas with a
high Catholic population—and the Government has been
accused of discriminating against these areas in its new industries drive—but it is fair to say that they tend to be the less
accessible border areas.

The major segregation is in housing and schools, and they
are interrelated. The initial segregation was a product of the
Plantation, and the Catholics' economic inferiority (which
reinforces segregation) stems in part from the fact that they were
driven on to the poorer land. In rural areas, there seems to be
little change in the geographical disposition of Protestants and
Catholics, for each side tends to hold on to its land. In urban
areas, there are recognised quarters, and names like Irish
Street, Scotch Street and English Street recur. The building
of Catholic churches and schools has tended to preserve the
geographical unity of these quarters. New housing estates have
not greatly altered the position; Catholics tend to be allocated
housing close to their existing ghettoes, which is not only convenient for them but preserves the political balance of the area.

As the 1969 disturbances indicated, there are real dangers in
breaking out of the ghettoes or blurring the lines between them.
Both Catholics living in predominantly Protestant streets in
Belfast, and Protestants living in predominantly Catholic
streets, found themselves subject to intimidation and petrol
bomb attacks. Their houses were often burned after they had
vacated them. In some towns, the gradual occupation of a
traditionally Protestant street by Catholics is an indication
that the street is past its best days. Protestants tend to assume
an attitude of superiority, and the proud inhabitants of a
new Protestant estate will describe the untidiness and squalor
of a neighbouring Catholic estate. If there is an element of
truth in this, reasons can be found in the Catholics' lower

economic status, in their larger families, and simply in a different attitude to what is important in life.

In one sense, the religious barriers are lowest in Belfast.
This is a product of urban anonymity, of the greater sophisti-
cation of the city and the fact that there are other things to
concentrate on, and of the fact that Protestants and Catholics
are inevitably thrown together more often. But, at the level of
society represented by the Falls, Shankill and Crumlin Roads,
it would seem from the 1969 disturbances that there has been
no easement. Rural areas fall somewhere between these two
extremes of city life. People are known to each other, and
qualities of neighbourliness must be preserved, even if there
are issues (not discussed when Protestant and Catholic meet
casually) on which they divide.

Attitudes have probably hardened in recent years in the
border areas, where many Unionists distrust O'Neillite liberal-
ism, but it is a fact that these areas survived the I.R.A. campaign of 1956–62 without internal strife. Social contacts are
limited, of course, and the Orange Order has its Catholic
parallel in the Ancient Order of Hibernians. The Catholics
have always resented the B Specials, who were a brusque
reminder that real power lay with the Protestants. But there is
generally an attitude of "live and let live", and farmers will
help each other regardless of religious differences. Provincial
towns are not dissimilar, except that the religious groups are
clustered together more and may not know so well their
neighbours of a different religion. Much depends on how even
the balance of Protestant and Catholic numbers is, and tensions
are greatest where it is felt that Unionists hold power by gerrymandering and by curbing Catholic prospects so that power
will not ultimately change hands. The larger the town, though,
the more likely it is that there is an upper class in which
Protestants and Catholics mix amicably.

Educational segregation is almost complete at primary and
secondary school level, but Protestants and Catholics come
together at university and some other levels of further education—though not at teacher training colleges. The National

Opinion Polls survey in 1967 asked whether Protestants and Catholics should be educated separately or together. About two-thirds of the electorate favoured desegregation in both primary and secondary schools, and this level of support was very evenly maintained throughout the different denominations.

In recent years, it has become more common for Unionists to say that Catholic insistence on separate schools is an obstacle to better community relations, but little real attempt has been made to explore the possibility of changing the existing pattern. In fact, a 1968 Education Act provided for increasing grants to voluntary schools from 65 per cent to 80 per cent, provided they accepted "maintained" status; this empowered the Ministry of Education to nominate one-third of a voluntary grammar school's governors, and local education authorities to act similarly for secondary moderns. Although the Catholic bishops were initially critical of the new scheme, and particularly of the increased powers given to Unionist-controlled local education authorities, they have agreed to give the scheme a trial.

The history of education in Northern Ireland has been a stormy one, and it would be unfair to suggest that the pressure for segregation comes solely from the Catholic side. The Protestant Churches have also pressed claims about the importance of religious teaching in schools, and many Protestants would have reservations about a system of state education in which their children were much of the time being taught by Catholics. The Protestants have also lobbied strongly for Government aid to voluntary schools, though they confined themselves largely to the established grammar schools and were prepared to cede voluntary primary schools to local education authorities.

An attempt was made by the Government in the 1920s to provide a secular education which might have allowed Protestants and Catholics to be schooled together, but this was thwarted by a united education committee of the three main Protestant Churches together with a committee of the Grand Orange Lodge of Ireland. The state schools (including those which were now handed over by Protestant school managers) became, in effect, Protestant schools. Thereafter, Catholics felt that the Government had recognised the Protestants' claims of conscience, but had not (despite embarking on aid to voluntary schools) treated Catholics' claims of conscience as generously.

The Catholic insistence on separate schools stems from a belief that education is an integral part of religious upbringing, and that only a Catholic school can provide the right atmosphere. The Church itself is unyielding on this, and on occasions members of the hierarchy have replied quite sharply to calls for desegregation—suggesting, even, that the Government has considered seriously an imposed takeover. Catholic educationists take a similar stand, and are probably worried about their career prospects in a state system. Both groups tend to say that separate education has no divisive effect, and that an improvement in community relations would be effected more readily by eliminating Catholic grievances. In a just society, the argument goes, it would not matter whether or not the two communities were educated together.

The case cannot easily be proved either way, and it is disappointing that there has not been research to measure the effects of segregated education—or, indeed, to determine how successfully separate Catholic education does achieve its objectives. It may be that separate education is not a prime cause of Northern Ireland's religious strife, but it must contribute to the two communities' continued ignorance of each other.

One particular issue should also be mentioned—the teaching of Irish history. Protestant schools have tended to teach English history, with Ireland examined mainly in its effect on its larger neighbour. Catholic schools pay more attention to the subject, and give it a nationalistic flavour. Overall, the teaching of Irish history has undoubtedly improved in recent years—a notable series of B.B.C. schools broadcasts helped— but there are still substantial differences of outlook.

It would be wrong to overemphasise the division between

Northern Ireland's two religious communities. It is deep but not absolute. What has happened in recent years is that, as the two communities have drawn together, there has remained in each a section which has not been educated to a new tolerance and has been frightened by the apparent collapse of old verities. This has been particularly the case in the Protestant community, not least because—as in the past—there has been a demagogic cleric to encourage their fears. Segregation in education has been modified to the extent that more deliberate efforts are made to encourage contacts between Protestant and Catholic schools—in appropriate sports, in debating contests and the like. The sharp increase in the university population has brought together more and more young people of different denominations—young people who are the future leaders of society.

The ecumenical movement has had its effect, particularly in fostering contacts between clergy of different denominations, and outbreaks of violence have also persuaded them to work together as never before. Indeed, the peace committees which have emerged in many areas must have a long-term effect in drawing Protestants and Catholics together—and, in many cases, at the street level at which the sectarian problem is most acute. Just as the best-educated escape the initial schools segregation, so the more affluent Catholics are less likely to live in ghettoes. But for the mass of people, it is probably in work that the best opportunities for mixing occur. One of the achievements of trade union leaders was to avoid serious strife on the shop floor in 1969, and moves towards fair employment practices in public bodies will increase the number of points at which Protestant and Catholic must learn to work side by side. It is at least a beginning.

6. *After Callaghan*

Before leaving Northern Ireland, James Callaghan had appealed for the barriers to come down in Belfast and Londonderry. Major Chichester-Clark renewed this appeal the following morning, and Eddie McAteer said: "The barricades have served their purpose wonderfully well, but are now a punishment only to our people." But behind the barricades there was still fear and suspicion, and Catholics were not yet ready to accept guarantees of protection by the British Army. In the Shankill Road area, late on Saturday night, a group of Protestants met to practise on their massive Lambeg drums, the tribal rhythms audible across no-man's-land. Posters were put up in many parts of Belfast warning: "Ulster is facing a Republican takeover".

The Unionist Parliamentary Party and executive officers of the Ulster Unionist Council met for three hours on Tuesday, 2 September, and a statement issued afterwards was notable for making no mention of the Home Secretary or the proposals announced in the communiqué. It merely indicated full support for "the Prime Minister and the Government in their efforts to establish stability in the community" and called on all sections to work together to play their part in building a new future for Northern Ireland. That night, a new barricade was erected by Protestants on Donegall Road, close to the end of the M1 motorway. Milk vans were brought into the barricades, and a contractor's truck had its tyres let down; on top was a Union Jack. But Protestants and Catholics living in the area had been working closely together, and it seemed outsiders might have been responsible.

During the week, other Protestant barricades were erected, apparently in protest at the Army's unwillingness to move against Catholic barricades. The Army did, however, act against barricades which were impeding traffic on some of the more important thoroughfares. The Government made it clear that, in the interests of the city's commercial life, main routes must remain open. But tension was clearly rising as the weekend approached, and on Friday Chichester-Clark appealed for calm. "I cannot believe that the building of barricades represents the will of the mass of the people of this city," he said, "nor can I believe that any responsible person can countenance any possibility of further violence and disorder."

On Sunday, troops used tear-gas in Belfast for the first time. It began with some jeering as a Catholic family evacuated a house in Beverley Street, between the Shankill Road and Divis Street. A Catholic crowd moved in to protect the family, while the Protestants were summoned by pirate radio to prevent "rebels and Republicans" invading the Shankill. The Army found itself separating hostile crowds in Percy Street, which links Shankill Road and Divis Street. The Catholics dispersed at the request of the Army and their own stewards, but tear-gas had to be used against the Protestants. As the news spread through the city, Protestants from the Sandy Row area seized army barricades of wood and barbed wire and carried them back to their own area, blocking traffic along a major route. The Army were suddenly unpopular, and it was announced that the R.U.C. would take sole responsibility for the Shankill and Sandy Row areas.

The ninth victim of the disturbances was a 29-year-old Protestant vigilante, Jack Todd, who was shot around 4.0 a.m. on Monday, 8 September. He died in Alloa Street, in a mixed Protestant–Catholic area north of the Crumlin Road. The shooting followed a meeting of two groups of vigilantes, and Todd was apparently shot from a Catholic house which was empty when searched. Catholics in the area immediately began to evacuate their houses, some under threat of being burned out. The following day, the Minister of Home Affairs,

Robert Porter, announced the setting-up of a Public Protection Authority which would operate around the clock. "Intimidation," he said, "is one of the most prevalent and certainly the most cowardly and despicable of the crimes to which the present situation has given rise." Petrol bomb attacks continued to be an almost nightly occurrence. (Porter was later to introduce a Bill giving magistrates power to impose two-year sentences for intimidation and petrol bomb offences.) The community conference—which had been meeting regularly since Chichester-Clark's peace conference on 18 August —called for a curfew in parts of Belfast and an 8.0 p.m. closing of public houses and licensed clubs.

On 9 September, Chichester-Clark again broadcast to the people of Northern Ireland. "The present situation in the city of Belfast cannot be allowed to continue. Ordinary life is being paralysed. Irresponsible broadcasts stir up new hatred. Above all, the many barricades are strangling the whole community. We cannot and we will not tolerate any further drift into anarchy. An elected Government is not going to surrender its authority to a mischief-making minority which has a minimum of real support."

The Prime Minister outlined his Government's reform programme, and said that all legitimate demands were being met. Only fear of actual physical harm, he said, justified keeping up the barricades. He then announced that he and General Freeland had agreed that the Army would erect and man a firm peace-line between the Divis Street area and the Shankill Road, on a line to be determined by a representative body from the City Hall. "In conjunction with this action, barricades will be removed in all areas of Belfast, both Protestant and Catholic, starting on the fringe of the city and moving into the centre. Where there is still genuine fear, military or police guards or patrols will be present." Chichester-Clark added that certain areas of Belfast would be blocked to traffic during the hours of darkness, and appealed: "Bring the barricades down. Start tonight or start tomorrow, but at any rate start quickly."

The following day, the Royal Engineers began building what was soon called Belfast's Berlin Wall. It stretched from Cupar Street to Coates Street, and largely consisted of iron stakes and barbed wire. Robert Porter made an order under the Special Powers Act banning traffic from an area between Crumlin Road and Grosvenor Road from 9.0 p.m. to 6.0 a.m. He also said he had no intention of invoking the Act against anyone involved in erecting or maintaining the barricades, though there would be normal prosecutions where there was evidence of law-breaking. It was announced that another 600 men of the Light Infantry were to augment the 5,000 troops already in Northern Ireland. But the barricades remained.

A three-man deputation from the Central Citizens' Defence Committee, representing Catholic districts throughout Belfast, went to the Home Office to seek assurances that the barricades would not be removed forcibly. Then, on Thursday, Gerry Fitt led a five-man deputation in discussions with the Home Secretary. It was agreed that, before barricades were removed, the local Army commander should discuss the situation with representatives of the people behind the barricades, so that the necessary protection could be assured. Another turbulent weekend raised Catholic fears, and troops and police had to form a barrier between hostile mobs in the New Lodge Road area; there were a number of petrol bomb attacks in different parts of the city. Two soldiers were also shot dead, but one turned out to be a suicide, and the other death had no connection with the disturbances.

On Monday, 15 September, a statement from the Central Defence Committee said that as part of any future negotiations with the Army on the removal of barricades, there would have to be discussion of such matters as the disarming and disbandment of the B Specials, the repeal of the Special Powers Act, and the disarming and reorganisation of the R.U.C. General Freeland flew out to talks at Downing Street, and the Ulster Cabinet met, after which a statement was issued insisting that the barricades come down. There were clearly divided views behind the barricades, and the Central Defence Committee retreated from what had seemed an intransigent position. The Army began to use persuasion with some success, and the Catholic Bishop of Down and Connor, Dr William Philbin, toured West Belfast. "For God's sake, if you want to put yourself in the right, take them down," he pleaded, but many Catholics were ready to argue with him.

Clearly, there was still a good deal of fear, but it was also evident that many Catholics were feeling the strain of life behind the barricades and looked for some return to normality. Some of the more active Republicans in the area had naturally emerged as leaders—Jim Sullivan, the chairman of the Central Defence Committee, was interned during the I.R.A. campaign in the 1950s—and possibly saw the barricades as a bargaining card they were unwilling to give up. There was some criticism of the role of Dr Philbin—and of Father Patrick Murphy, a heavily built priest who had accompanied Gerry Fitt to London. But the clergy seemed ultimately to have a better feeling for the situation, and the barricades slowly began to come down with the help of Army bulldozers. Troops remained on guard, but there was no suggestion that police would be allowed back.

Meanwhile, the report of the Cameron Commission had been published on Friday, 12 September, and had possibly contributed to the weekend's disturbances. The report was by implication highly critical of successive Unionist Governments for not alleviating Catholic grievances, which it found to be well documented. The Government, for its part, accepted the report. To militant Protestants, it was one more example of a weak Government failing to defend traditional Unionist policies.

The report covered the period from the Caledon squatting incident and the subsequent Dungannon march on 24 August 1968, to the Londonderry disturbances of 19–20 April. It divided the causes of disorders into two categories, general and particular. The general causes were:

(1) A rising sense of continuing injustice and grievance among large sections of the Catholic population, in particular in Londonderry and Dungannon, in respect of inadequate

housing provision by some local authorities; unfair methods of allocating houses, and refusal to adopt a points system; and misuse of discretionary powers of allocating houses to perpetuate Unionist control.

(2) Complaints, now well documented in fact, of discrimination against Catholics in local government appointments, especially in senior posts.

(3) Complaints, again well documented, of deliberate manipulation of local government electoral boundaries or of refusal to apply for necessary extensions, to ensure Unionist control.

(4) A growing and powerful sense of resentment and frustration among Catholics that the Government would not accept the need to investigate these complaints or provide and enforce a remedy for them.

(5) Resentment, particularly among Catholics, of the existence of the B Specials as a partisan and para-military force recruited exclusively from Protestants.

(6) Widespread resentment among Catholics in particular of regulations made under the Special Powers Act, and of the Act itself.

(7) Fears and apprehensions among Protestants of a threat to Unionist domination and control of Government by increase of Catholic population and powers. These were inflamed in particular by the activities of the Ulster Constitution Defence Committee and the Ulster Protestant Volunteers, and provoked strong hostile reaction to civil rights claims, leading to physical violence against civil rights demonstrators.

Among particular causes, the report noted strong popular resentment of the ministerial ban on the 5 October march; without this ban, the numbers taking part would probably have been small and the situation could have been safely handled by available police forces. William Craig was criticised, not only for the original ban, but for a subsequent ban on meetings within Derry's walls; the latter could not be enforced, and was therefore not only useless but mischievous. There was also criticism of the civil rights movement for ineffective control of the demonstrations in Derry on 5 October and in Newry on

11 January, while the commission found that the Civil Rights Association had soon been infiltrated by subversive left-wing and revolutionary elements which provoked violence and disorder in the guise of supporting a non-violent movement.

There was particular criticism of three leaders of the People's Democracy movement—Eamonn McCann, Michael Farrell and Cyril Toman. "We believe, not only from the evidence of these gentlemen—who are in the forefront of the movement—but also from the unchallengeable facts of the events themselves, that those leaders, dedicated as they are to extreme left wing political opinions and objectives, are determined to channel People's Democracy in directions of their choice and in so doing are prepared and ready—where and when they consider it suits them—to invoke and accept violence." Of Bernadette Devlin, the commission said: "We do not doubt the sincerity with which she holds her views—which, as it appears to us, are directed substantially to the redress of what she regards as social and economic injustices and inequalities—but we do think that she would not rule out the use of force to achieve her own purposes if other methods of political persuasion had, in her judgment, failed." The Cameron report perhaps failed to assess the strength of the left-wing revolutionaries, but it had no doubt that it presented a real danger. "Whatever may be the real capacity for leadership possessed by any of those whom we have named or their power to influence and control a body of marchers or demonstrators, there is no doubt that they represent and propagate political ideas which (1) are far more politically extreme than the objects for which the Civil Rights Association has campaigned and (2) represent a threat to the stability and existence of the Northern Ireland Constitution."

The commission also criticised Paisley and Bunting:

In the face of the mass of evidence from both police and civilian sources as to the extent to which the supporters of Dr Paisley and Major Bunting were armed at Armagh and on the occasion of the People's Democracy march to

Londonderry, it is idle to pretend that these were peacefully directed protest meetings. On neither occasion were the Civil Rights or People's Democracy marchers armed; on neither occasion had they offered violence towards others; on neither occasion was the march or demonstration routed through streets or areas traditionally Protestant or "loyalist"; on neither occasion were provocative banners or emblems flown, carried or displayed.

The report added:

Both these gentlemen and the organisations with which they are so closely and authoritatively concerned must, in our opinion, bear a heavy share of direct responsibility for the disorders in Armagh and at Burntollet Bridge and also for inflaming passions and engineering opposition to lawful, and what would in all probability otherwise have been peaceful, demonstrations or at least have attracted only modified and easily controlled opposition.

Finally, the police came under fire. Their handling of the 5 October demonstration was "in certain material respects ill co-ordinated and inept". There was unauthorised and irregular use of batons at an early stage, and there seemed to have been neither reason nor excuse for the "indiscriminate use of water cannon on pedestrians on the Craigavon Bridge". The commission found that the available police forces had not provided adequate protection at Burntollet or at Irish Street, Londonderry, on 4 January. Moreover, a number of policemen were guilty that night of "misconduct which involved assault and battery, malicious damage to property in streets in the predominantly Catholic Bogside area giving reasonable cause for apprehension of personal injury among other innocent inhabitants, and the use of provocative sectarian and political slogans". The commission also noted that it had been presented with a considerable body of evidence to establish further acts of grave misconduct by police on 19–20 April, and said it was in the interest of police and public that these should be rigorously probed.

It should be added that nine days earlier the Inspector-General of the R.U.C., Anthony Peacocke, had announced that 16 policemen were to be disciplined for misconduct during the January disturbances at Burntollet and Derry. This followed the report of County Inspector Baillie, who had in fact recommended that criminal prosecutions be considered in two cases. The Attorney-General had decided not to prefer criminal charges, in the light of the Prime Minister's amnesty. The Baillie report was not published, but the Cameron Commission said it had reached the same conclusions from the evidence presented to it.

There was little or nothing of significance in the Cameron report which an intelligent reader of newspapers would not have known or concluded, but its publication was a traumatic experience for the Unionists. Chichester-Clark looked visibly shaken at a Press conference called on the day of publication. "It is self-evident," he said, "that in the past all of us have made mistakes." His message, which he was to repeat on other occasions, was that there should be no recriminations and that people should now look to the future. A Government commentary published with the Cameron report had little to say about the reasons for the civil rights movement's existence, and ended by asking for "the active support and co-operation of every member of the community and for the rejection by every responsible body and every responsible person of the hostile, revolutionary and subversive elements which have been seeking to destroy the constitutional structure of the State—as has now been amply demonstrated by the Cameron Report".

With the left-wing revolutionaries as convenient scapegoats, it was possible to avoid facing up to the problem of Protestant extremism or to the nature of Unionist politics as Catholics had so long experienced it. The Cameron report, by contrast, had been complimentary to the civil rights movement, saying it would be a grave political and social error to regard it as narrowly sectarian or subversively political. "We disagree profoundly, having heard much evidence, with the view which professes to see agitation for civil rights as a mere pretext for other and more subversive activities."

The Prime Minister quickly received a vote of confidence from the Unionist Party executive, but it was obvious that some members of the party would feel the report should have been rejected. Craig, who had been criticised for refusing to to give evidence, described its assessment of some situations as naïve; Desmond Boal, the member for Shankill, called it an enormous damp squib. John Hume, praised by Cameron as responsible and capable, said that Craig was so discredited by the report that he should leave public life immediately. Eamonn McCann described the report as under-researched and overwritten; Major Bunting said that if defending the realm was inflammatory, then even General Freeland might face that charge. Ian Paisley, visiting America, said that Terence O'Neill had refused to allow a public sworn inquiry so that Catholics could bring charges without having to substantiate them. Returning home, he warmed to his subject at an open-air meeting in the County Down village of Crossgar. He called for 100,000 Protestants to go to Stormont when the report was being debated, and said: "We will show these compromising, fence-sitting Unionists that there are still Protestants in this country not prepared to compromise." On 20 September, he held a rally at Burntollet, and warned that if the Government continued its policy of selling out Protestants, there would be such "an affair in Ulster that all the restraining voice I might raise will no longer be heeded".

The political temperature rose, but the barricades continued to come down, and few remained in Belfast when the British Defence Secretary, Denis Healey, arrived for a brief visit on 18 September. During his visit, the Derry Citizens' Defence Association announced that its barricades would also be removed, but that neither the R.U.C. nor the B Specials would be allowed to enter Bogside and the military would do so only by invitation. A white line replaced the barricades, but new tension returned to Derry on Wednesday, 24 September, when fighting broke out between Protestant and Catholic teenagers in the Strand Road area. It spread towards the centre of the city, and 55-year-old William King, a Protestant, was killed. It appeared that he had been anxious about the safety of his teenage son, and the Northern Ireland state pathologist said after a quick post-mortem that a heart condition had contributed to King's death. Many Protestants felt that the troops had not moved in quickly enough to save the dead man, but military cordons were effective in preventing a second night of violence and the situation gradually eased.

The only light relief was provided by the propaganda battle which had begun when Bernadette Devlin slipped out of Bogside towards the end of August, crossed the border into Co. Donegal, and flew to the United States. Her objective was to raise one million dollars for the relief of victims of the August disturbances, and she was soon being photographed with Mayor John Lindsay of New York, who had presented the mini-skirted traveller with the key of the city. She met U Thant, Secretary General of the United Nations, and appeared successfully on television. In the end, though, she cut her visit short without reaching her financial target. It seemed that the Irish Americans who first welcomed her had realised that she was as critical of Dublin's Tories as of those at Stormont. They had also realised that Miss Devlin was sponsored by the National Association for Irish Justice, an American organisation linked to such militant organisations as the Black Panthers and the Students for a Democratic Society.

Much was made of these links by Unionist M.P.s who pursued Miss Devlin to the United States. Where once she had been Tariq Ali in a trouser suit, she became Fidel Castro in a mini-skirt. Robin Bailie and Stratton Mills told a Press conference in New York that the People's Democracy aimed to establish a Socialist Irish republic—"something on the lines of Cuba". They saw events in Northern Ireland as part of a wider pattern of revolution. Ian Paisley also visited the United States—collecting for the relief of Protestants—and Frank Gogarty arrived to collect more money. Captain Laurence Orr, leader of the Westminster Unionists, visited

Canada. In Belfast, the Unionists launched a fund-raising drive, and issued a booklet called *Ulster—The Facts*, which was described by Mr Justice Scarman as "unfortunate in its timing and its authority".

Meanwhile, the Dublin Government continued to take an active interest in Northern affairs. George Colley, the Minister for Industry and Commerce, said on a visit to Canada that his Government was more determined than ever to renegotiate Northern Ireland's status with the British Government. At the United Nations, an attempt to put the Ulster situation on the agenda of the General Assembly failed. Kevin Boland, the Minister for Local Government, accused the British Government of deliberately deciding to "perpetuate injustice to our country". But the most moderate and statesmanlike contribution came from Prime Minister Lynch at a dinner in Tralee on 20 September.

He said that, in seeking the reunification of Ireland, his Government's aim was not to extend the domination of Dublin. "We have many times down the years expressed our willingness to seek a solution on federal lines. . . . Whatever the constitutional setting might be—and we are prepared to explore all the possibilities in constructive discussion—the united Ireland we desire is one in which there would be a scrupulously fair deal for all." He said it was unnecessary to repeat that they sought reunification by peaceful means. They were not seeking to overthrow by violence the Stormont Parliament or Government, but rather to win the agreement of a sufficient number of people in the North to an acceptable form of reunification. He said the Stormont Government, as the executive instrument of a subordinate parliament, could not receive formal international recognition, but there were many fruitful contacts in matters of mutual concern. He quoted Craigavon's words: "In this island, we cannot live always separated from one another. We are too small to be apart or for the border to be there for all time."

Interviewed about his Tralee speech, Lynch said that Article 44 of the Irish Constitution, which recognised the

"special position" of the Catholic Church, was an apparent
obstacle to unity. He said he had not made up his mind about
holding a referendum, which would be necessary for an
amendment of the Constitution, but it soon became clear that
there was substantial support for a change. Cardinal Conway
said he would not shed a tear if the relevant sub-sections of the
article disappeared, and he noted that the Catholic Church
enjoyed no legal privilege whatever. But Article 44 was
probably of less importance to Northern Protestants than the
prohibitions on divorce and contraceptives and the Republic's
claim in the Constitution to exercise jurisdiction over 32
counties. Major Chichester-Clark made no reference to Article
44 in a thoughtful reply to Lynch's speech. It was the former's
most restrained comment since the August troubles, and significantly it emerged after a time-lag of three days.

The Ulster Premier did single out the article asserting
sovereignty over all Ireland, and said that good relations would
not be advanced by stationing troops along the border or by
seeking U.N. action or by waging a propaganda war. "I am
not saying that Mr Lynch and his colleagues have not a
perfect right to express the hope that one day North and
South will move into a closer agreed relationship. But it is
incompatible with this approach to lay present and unacceptable claims to the territory under our jurisdiction, and to use
every opportunity on the international stage to harass and
embarrass us."

But there were hints in the reply that the Northern Premier
might be ready to examine federal solutions in which Britain
had a part to play. "Indeed, there is no reason," he said, "why
North and South under two parliaments should not wherever
possible work together, not only for the good of Ireland but for
the good of these islands as a whole." He said that no really
satisfactory and statesmanlike view of the future could be
found except in the context of the British Isles as a whole,
very probably in increasingly close association with the rest
of Europe. Chichester-Clark described Northern Ireland in
terms unusual from a Unionist more accustomed to insisting

that Ulster was British. "Whatever our failings, we represent a bridge between this island and its neighbour."

Chichester-Clark went on to get the general endorsement of his parliamentary party for the Government's reform programme, then got the support of the party's standing committee. He appointed a liberal Unionist, Dr Robert Simpson, as Minister of Community Relations: Simpson immediately resigned from the Orange and Masonic orders. But there was still an air of tension, and the results of the arms amnesty had been disappointing. As the end of September approached, Porter extended the ban on public processions and meetings for a further three months, and included all outdoor meetings. The new terms of the ban would have included Paisley's Burntollet rally. Again, only the Salvation Army was excluded; even Remembrance Day parades were affected, as was a traditional parade of Apprentice Boys in Derry in December.

On Saturday, 27 September, an organisation called the Ulster Loyalist Association held a noisy rally in the Ulster Hall to celebrate the 57th anniversary of the signing of the Ulster Covenant. William Craig, the principal speaker, said: "We do not want to have to emulate the example of those who signed the Covenant in 1912. Let it be clear that if necessary we will." He accused the Governments in Belfast and London of political blundering, and said the reform package had been put forward as if it had been won by rioting and disorder in the street. He ended by saying: "On many other occasions in this hall, people concluded that Ulster had spoken. May that be so tonight."

Ulster spoke again at midnight. Three men making their way home from Sandy Row to the Shankill Road area were halted by the Army as they got to the Townsend Street peaceline. There were angry words, and Protestant and Catholic crowds quickly gathered. Before long, stones, bricks and petrol bombs were being thrown across the peaceline. Protestants attacked Coates Street, where the peace-line ended, and burned down several houses. The Army replied with tear-gas, and the Protestant mob moved towards the Catholic flats at

Unity Walk, throwing petrol bombs on to the balconies. Shots were fired in reply. It was 3.0 a.m. before the crowds dispersed, and there was more fighting later in the morning when petrol bombs were thrown at an Elim Pentecostal church in Melbourne Street, close to Coates Street, while a service was in progress. Again the Army used tear-gas.

On Monday, Craig told a Young Unionist rally that the whole country was crying out for swift, firm action. He said that firearms should have been used by police in Londonderry on 12 August to clear the mob from the top of the Bogside flats. The Protestant temper was rising, and although fewer than 10,000 joined Paisley's protest at Stormont the following day, it was the most turbulent demonstration ever staged there. The crowd was good-humoured at first, but its mood changed and reporters and cameramen were threatened. Both Opposition Members and liberal Unionists were jostled as they arrived, and there were complaints to the Speaker in the Commons, who gave unavailing orders to clear the main lobby. Small numbers of demonstrators had been allowed into the building to lobby their M.P.s, and one threw tea at John Hume and Ivan Cooper. William Craig appeared on a balcony above the crowd, and was loudly cheered. The crowd waved Union Jacks and sang Orange songs.

Within the House, the Government presented four of its reform Bills, and moved on to the Cameron report. Chichester-Clark said they were beginning probably the most crucial series of sittings Stormont had ever known. "We can take it as an opportunity to begin to mould the future to a better pattern," he said, "or we can look back into the past and irretrievably lose our way." But the subsequent debate showed that the attitudes of individual M.P.s had changed little. The speeches made might, in essence, have been heard any time during the preceding years. But at least the Opposition M.P.s, feeling that Cameron had vindicated their criticisms of Unionist rule, had all decided to give up their boycott.

There was another weekend of violence. On Saturday night, a Protestant girl ran across the Albert Bridge from the

Catholic Markets area and claimed she had been beaten. Police and soldiers cordoned off a Protestant crowd as it advanced towards the bridge. On Sunday afternoon, Paisley conducted an Orange service in his newly opened Martyrs' Memorial church in East Belfast. Early in the afternoon, a crowd attempted to form a procession in defiance of Porter's ban, and was partly dispersed by tear-gas. After the service, the crowd swept past police and a line of troops attempting to put up a barbed-wire cordon, but was halted at Albert Bridge by armoured cars and Land Rovers with gas-masked troops.

Later in the night, there was fighting between troops and Protestants in East Belfast. Shots were fired at soldiers there and in the Donegall Road area, on the other side of the city. The Army's newly formed snatch squads—equipped with batons, steel helmets, gas-masks and bullet-proof vests—were in action, seeking out ringleaders among the angry mobs. On Monday night, a Shankill Road mob attempted to march on the Unity Walk flats, but was thwarted by troops, police and even B Specials, who had been brought back unarmed to patrol the Shankill. The situation remained tense, but Catholic barricades which had gone up the previous weekend began to come down again, because the Catholics were satisfied with the Army's handling of the weekend's incidents. The Citizens' Defence Committee agreed to military policemen patrolling the Falls Road area. On Monday, incidentally, the report of the inquiry into the use of CS gas in Derry was published. It found that no healthy person had developed any illness as a result, but recommended that agents of this kind should be studied from the same point of view as a new drug, with particular reference to those who might be inadvertently exposed to it.

On the eve of Callaghan's return to Northern Ireland, Terence O'Neill made one of his few political interventions since giving up the premiership. The occasion was the decision of Richard Ferguson, the liberally minded young Unionist M.P. for South Antrim, to resign his seat. His constituency association had passed a vote of no confidence following his resignation from the Orange order, and he said he had been advised that to continue the fight to maintain a liberal view-point within the party would place an intolerable strain on his health. "Let us make no mistake about it," O'Neill said in a grim statement. "He was badgered and bullied into this decision by the same sort of people who created those dis-graceful scenes at Stormont last week. If people like Dick Ferguson, who would be welcome as Conservative candidates in Britain, can have no place in our public life here, then the future of democracy in this province is dark indeed." The Home Secretary himself said it was an appalling disgrace that a young M.P. should be driven out by extremists in his own party, and added: "Such an action forfeits tremendous support on the other side of the water."

Callaghan's second visit to Northern Ireland was less dramatic than his first, for he spent much of the time in discussions with the Government, but the outcome was equally far-reaching. He arrived on Wednesday evening, 8 October, and said at a Press conference: "I think it is important that citizens in Northern Ireland should recognise that there is no going back on the interest that Westminster has in the affairs of this country. For good or for ill, and I hope it is for the good of all the people of Northern Ireland, there will be a close and continuing interest in what takes place here in all its constitu-tional and political aspects."

The Hunt report was published on Friday morning. It recommended that the B Specials should be disbanded, and that the regular police should be relieved of all duties of a para-military nature as soon as possible. It recommended also that the use of firearms should be strictly limited, and that the R.U.C. should cease to have automatic weapons, self-loading rifles or armoured cars. Two new forces were recommended. One was to be a volunteer reserve force, to help in ordinary police duties. The other (subsequently called the Ulster Defence Regiment) was to be a part-time force, under the command of the British Army G.O.C., which would help troops protect key installations and guard against threats to the security of the Six Counties. The committee said the R.U.C. reserve force—the riot squad which had borne the brunt of physical violence and a great deal of criticism—should be renamed the special patrol group. One-third of the force should be replaced each year, and no officer should command it for more than three years.

The Hunt committee also said the police should come under a new police authority, whose membership would reflect the proportions of different groups in the community, particularly Catholics. The authority would have a particular duty to keep itself informed on how complaints against the police were dealt with—and new procedures on English lines were recommended for investigating complaints. The R.U.C. would be inspected at least once a year by Her Majesty's Inspectorate of Constabulary. The practice of reserving one-third of the vacancies in the R.U.C. for Catholics should be discontinued—in fact, only 11 per cent of police were Catholics—but vigorous efforts should be made to increase the number of Catholic entrants. The report said that the closure of some small police stations in difficult urban areas and in some rural areas should be reconsidered; two areas singled out were Bogside and Cullingtree Road, Belfast. It recommended that sergeants and constables should wear numbers throughout Northern Ireland, and made a number of proposals to link the R.U.C. with police forces in Great Britain. It was also recommended that the R.U.C.'s uniform should change from dark green to blue, as "the symbol most likely to convince the public that the role of the force has been changed".

On Friday morning, Chichester-Clark held a Press conference at which he said the Government had decided to adopt the main principles of the Hunt report—but on the basis of certain understandings and guarantees. These were that the disarming of the police must depend in practice upon assessment of the security situation; that, once constituted, the new security force should not be changed without the fullest consultation with the Northern Ireland Government; that the

B Specials should remain in being until a fully effective security force was available to replace them; that the vital interests of the Government in the defence of the province should be recognised by continuing arrangements for the fullest consultation as to policy for use of the new force; and that a fully adequate military garrison should be maintained with effective machinery for deploying units of the Army and the new security force.

It was clear that Callaghan had conceded nothing, and that the Hunt report was to be implemented in all essential points. The Premier had one further announcement: the Inspector-General, Anthony Peacocke, had resigned and would be succeeded by the Commissioner of the City of London Police, Sir Arthur Young. Later, Young announced that some policemen would be on patrol without arms the following day, and within a few days unarmed police were on duty (accompanied by military police) in Bogside and the Falls Road. Within a few weeks, police throughout Northern Ireland had voluntarily disarmed themselves.

A meeting of the Unionist Parliamentary Party was held in the afternoon, and gave general endorsement to the Hunt committee proposals by 28 votes to seven. Some members were absent, though, and it was clear that the party would want another opportunity to discuss the report. Then came the evening Press conference, with Callaghan revealing in a communiqué a further dose of controversial measures. The most striking was the decision to set up a central housing authority, which would take over full responsibility for public housing. This was put forward as an emergency measure to deal with an emergency situation—substantial housing shortages in many areas, and a higher proportion of outworn houses needing replacement than in England and Wales—but it had the additional effect of solving (more reliably than a points system) the problem of discriminatory housing allocations by local authorities. The communiqué went on to point out the consequent needs in such fields as road-building, water and sewerage and other facilities, and noted also that the administration of other services—health, welfare, child care, education and libraries—was under review. The outcome was a proposal to set up a broadly based review body to review the current proposals for local government reorganisation. In other words, the 17 areas which Opposition members had described as a new gerrymander were almost certainly to be scrapped.

The working parties on anti-discrimination legislation had also reported since Callaghan's last visit, and legislation to set up a Community Relations Commission and a Commissioner for Complaints (an ombudsman for local authorities and public bodies) was already before the Commons. But the communiqué revealed that the Government would introduce an anti-discrimination clause in all its contracts, and had agreed on measures to ensure fair practices in public employment; a local government staff commission would advise on the selection of candidates for senior appointments, and the idea of a commission to cover staffing throughout the public sector would be further studied. The one point at which there appeared to be hesitation was the possibility of legislation to outlaw incitement to religious hatred, which was merely to be kept under review.

The rest of the communiqué dealt with the economic situation, and announced a scheme of free compensation against damage and loss arising from riot or civil commotion, which would apply to new manufacturing projects. The rate of grants available to new industries was to be stepped up, and the Government would continue for an additional year the selective employment payment for male labour, which was soon to be discontinued in Britain's development areas. About 2,500 jobs would be provided by winter unemployment relief schemes. The British Government, it was clear, would provide whatever money was necessary "within the existing framework of financial arrangements between the two Governments".

At his Press conference, Callaghan said the reform package was surely adequate for all fair-minded people in the North. The only people who would find fault with it were a small bunch of violent trouble-makers. The trouble-makers were soon at work, and the same evening angry crowds milled around the Shankill Road area. A number of new barricades were erected, and bursts of automatic gunfire were heard during the night It was a prelude to Belfast's bloodiest night since the August riots.

Shankill Road is always crowded on a Saturday night. About eleven o'clock on 11 October, the crowd began to take shape in the lower Shankill, about Dover Street, not far from the Unity Walk flats. Police and B Specials in turn formed a barrier, four deep with linked arms. The Protestant mob, carrying Union Jacks, tried to break through the police cordon. They were momentarily repulsed, and the police drew back to regroup. A platoon of soldiers moved in, and the first canisters of CS gas exploded. As the crowd scattered to escape the fumes, snipers began to fire, and 29-year-old Constable Victor Arbuckle dropped to the ground. He died soon afterwards. Two other constables also fell, with gunshot wounds in their legs. More troops moved in, and CS gas dispersed the mob each time it regrouped. The sniping intensified, and the troops had to take cover, but the Army snatch squad was still able to make a number of arrests. Eventually, the troops were given the order to return fire, and two civilians were killed. It turned out that the dead men, 32-year-old Herbert Hawe and 25-year-old George Dickey, were cousins.

The rioters withdrew behind a barricade of overturned cars, but the troops eventually forced a way through with Saracen armoured cars. Each side street was carefully searched, and troops were stationed to cover the advance. The police were held back, although they would willingly have given assistance. Elsewhere in the city, there were outbursts of violence, as if in sympathy with the Shankill demonstrators. In Limestone Road, in North Belfast, troops halted a mob which attempted to march on a Catholic church. Across the river, a crowd stoned policemen in the Woodstock Road, and there was some sniping. Troops sealed off the Shore Road area of the city, which was threatened by a Protestant mob. It was dawn before Belfast was quiet, and by this time the Army had sealed off the Shankill. Road blocks had been strengthened, there were armoured cars at strategic points, and troops were manning barbed-wire barricades at almost every street corner. The casualty figures totalled 3 dead and 66 injured (including 3 police, 21 soldiers and 42 civilians). There were 69 arrests.

On Sunday, troops and police made a three-hour search of the Shankill area, and seized arms, ammunition, a pirate radio transmitter and propaganda material. A helicopter hovered above them, and warned residents: "If fire is opened up on us, we will return it." Chichester-Clark, looking drawn and unkempt, stumbled through a television broadcast. "As I have said, there is no danger either to the state or to the constitution, but let it be clear, far and away the greatest danger is acts of folly of a kind that took place last night. Folly of that kind is the real danger to Northern Ireland."

During the day, another 500 troops of the Parachute Regiment arrived in Belfast. At night, a Protestant crowd assembled on the Shankill Road, and new barricades were erected. An anti-tank pit was dug and filled with petrol and oil, which could be set alight if armoured cars attempted to pass. Some shots were fired, and the troops replied with tear-gas. Earlier in the day, Callaghan had been scheduled to address an audience of young people at Queen's University. He cancelled the meeting.

This is perhaps as good a point as any to end the narrative of Northern Ireland's revolution. It would obviously be a continuing story, with the province poised between reform and reaction. Callaghan returned to London on Monday, 13 October, to take part in a Commons debate which underlined the unity of views held by the Labour and Conservative front benches; the days when a Unionist Government could hope to have its shortcomings overlooked by its Conservative allies were gone. On Wednesday, John McKeague, chairman of the Shankill Defence Association, was jailed for his part in the attempted procession to Paisley's church on 5 October—the anniversary, ironically, of the banned Derry march.

At the weekend, a 7.0 p.m. curfew on drinking in Belfast was introduced, in the belief that drinking had contributed to disturbances in the past, and the city had its quietest weekend for months. There was mounting criticism of the Government's acceptance of the Hunt report—some B Specials resigned, and votes of no confidence were passed by a few Unionist associations—and William Craig warned that, if the Government continued on its present course, it would lead to "violence and bloodshed of the worst order". Chichester-Clark attempted, rather unconvincingly, to take the line that the B Specials were not really being disbanded. "True, their name and organisation will change," he said, "but that has been the fate of many fine regiments in the British Army too." The Premier did, however, get an encouraging vote of support (almost 5–1) for himself, his Government and their reform policies at a critical Unionist Council meeting on 25 October. It seemed that the realities of the Northern Ireland situation had begun to be recognised even by the grassroots of the Unionist Party.

But the U.V.F. remained active, and claimed responsibility for some bomb explosions in the Republic. On 19 October, a member of the illegal force died in an attempt to blow up a power station in Co. Donegal. This persuaded another member to turn Queen's evidence and reveal his part in explosions in the North in March and April; he was jailed for twelve years and, as the year ended, ten other Protestants awaited trial on charges of conspiring to cause explosions. On 22 December, Bernadette Devlin was sentenced to six months' imprisonment on charges arising from the battle of Bogside in August and immediately lodged an appeal. It seemed that the final outcome of these cases—and reaction to them—could have an effect on community peace in 1970. Terence O'Neill, whose political career had been so summarily ended, became a life peer in the New Year honours list.

7. *Future Tense*

The Irish problem is the Protestant problem. The Northern Ireland problem is the Protestant problem. Until the plantation of Ulster, the native Irish had absorbed and been absorbed by successive waves of immigrant peoples; the planters, fortified by their separate religion, largely remained aloof. Their descendants are still defending the original conquest. In another continent, they would be called white settlers.

The partition of Ireland was accomplished by force—or the threat of force. It is not likely that it will be removed by force —not, certainly, against the will of the majority in the North. The I.R.A. carries little weight on either side of the border, and if Jack Lynch was unwilling to send in his handful of troops to relieve Bogside, it is unlikely that any of his successors will be more aggressive. The British Government is prepared to use force to restore peace, to protect Northern Ireland from terrorist activity, and possibly (at some future date) to ensure that the will of the people is not frustrated by a recalcitrant Government at Stormont. For the moment, the fundamental fact is that a majority of the electorate in Northern Ireland are in favour of the British connection, and any change can come only with the acquiescence of that majority. The Catholic minority may force internal changes, most probably with the assistance of the British Government. It may improve its existence to the point where it can outvote the Protestants. But, for the moment, the Protestant viewpoint determines the major constitutional issue.

Would a united Ireland be the solution to the North's sectarian strife? Unionism would cease to have any political relevance. The Northern Protestants would be forced to rethink their position and come to terms with a new situation. They could find themselves politically impotent, when confronted by the Catholic majority within a 32-County Republic; but it is just as likely that they would hold a balance of power, and be wooed by the major parties now in the Republic. But a united Ireland is not in sight—certainly not as Nationalists have traditionally envisaged it—and it is doubtful if even a majority of Northern Catholics now want it.

Is the federal solution a possibility? Not, if the Northern Protestants are to decide the issue, in the manner envisaged by Lynch's Tralee speech. But it is worth recalling that the Crowther Commission may recommend a series of regional parliaments, and that something closer to a federal system may emerge in the United Kingdom. Would the Republic be prepared to sacrifice some of its sovereignty to participate in such a system, if it involved a united Ireland? Is formal partnership with England, the enemy of centuries, a practical possibility? There would have to be an appreciable shifting of opinion on both sides of the Irish border before agreement on these lines became possible, but it should not be ruled out. The prospect of both the United Kingdom and the Republic entering the European Economic Community suggests at least that North–South antagonisms cannot be allowed to continue.

Unfortunately, changes in people's attitudes in Northern Ireland tend to be inhibited by the constitutional question. The most useful step that might be taken at this stage would be to make provision for a periodic referendum on the question of union with Great Britain; indeed, it would be interesting to see the result of such a referendum, rather than having to rely on election results as an indication of how people really feel. A second step might be the reintroduction of proportional representation, so that some of the smaller political groupings had a better chance to win seats. If it helped ultimately to break the Unionists' long years of rule, it would enliven Ulster politics.

But the Unionists are not interested in creating conditions in which they would find themselves in Opposition, or forced to negotiate a coalition Government. Nor is it likely that the

British Government would intervene; Callaghan's role has been to impose standards of justice and equality on the Stormont administration, not to interfere with party politics. The question then is whether new political forces can arise to challenge the traditional dominance of the Unionists, or whether existing forces (including the Unionists themselves) can be regrouped.

O'Neill's political strategy was to shift the Unionist Party across and astride the traditional religious gulf, to embrace a proportion of Catholics and shed some of Unionism's traditional right wing supporters. The strategy failed, in the sense that he was unable to command sufficient Catholic votes during the 1969 general election, but it has not been abandoned. The more progressive Unionist leaders are still prepared to say that they hope for Catholic recruits to the party. But it is a strategy which assumes, and is directed towards, the continuation in power of the Unionist Party. A more fundamental improvement in Ulster politics would be to find a system which allowed power to alternate between two or more parties. This will not easily be achieved while Northern Ireland's constitutional position appears to be dependent on the outcome of each general election.

The success of the civil rights movement has provoked a good deal of self-examination on the Opposition side, and the outcome may be a more obviously radical party or coalition to oppose the conservatism of the Unionist Party. But, if this were largely Catholic in inspiration, it might make little or no impact on Protestant voters; the Unionist dominance would be confirmed. Such a move would be likely to split the Nationalist Party, some of whose members would not approve of the partition issue being subordinated to economic and social problems which were more immediately soluble. Their view, in any case, would be that a united Ireland is the only effective and permanent solution to these problems.

There is always a possibility of a Unionist split, for the party is still divided internally much as it was during O'Neill's premiership. There has been a reluctant acceptance of the reform programme, but undoubtedly issues will arise in the future to test the party's willingness to accept further changes.

The *ad hoc* organisations which supported pro-O'Neill independents are still largely in existence. The New Ulster Movement, a group of moderates, has a growing membership; it
describes itself as a political movement rather than a party, but
its members might have to opt for more direct action, particularly if they are driven out of the Unionist Party. One problem,
though, is that the New Ulster Movement embraces people
from a number of other parties, who might not be willing to
give up these allegiances if the N.U.M. became a political
party. The situation might be clarified if the right leader arose
to command the moderates, a leader who was able to persuade
the electorate that the important issue was not the border, but
the internal question of community relations. But the success of
such a move might depend on winning the support of some of
the present Unionist M.P.s.

What is Stormont's future? The present administration could
well be described as a puppet government, in that recently the
major policy initiatives have been imposed on it from outside.
It is anomalous that, while so many of the Opposition's long-
standing criticisms are now accepted as valid, the façade of
power remains with the party which for so long failed to tackle
the fundamental injustices in Ulster society. Parliament has
pressed ahead rapidly with the reform programme, but has not
improved as a debating chamber. In theory, Government and
Opposition were largely united in support of reforms, but traditional hostility has continued to assert itself. Nor has the Government much political expertise, yet this is abundantly needed to
chart a way through a tense situation.

Nor will the problems be confined to Parliament. The im-
plementation of reforms will present more problems than the
actual legislation, and the civil rights movement may well take
to the streets again. The menace of Protestant extremism is very
real, and the Ulster Volunteer Force could ultimately prove to be
well armed and fanatical in its resistance to change. The I.R.A.
seems a lesser danger, but it cannot be ignored. In an essentially
unstable situation, the presence of British troops is probably
required for months and even years.

What must be said is that the Stormont experiment in devolution has so far failed. Admittedly, there are some merits in
the present set-up, not least the accessibility of the whole
administration. Admittedly, the subordinate parliament could
hardly have been planted in more infertile ground. But by no
quantitative standards (levels of employment, average income
and the like) can it be deemed a success, and the scarred streets
patrolled by soldiers are evidence of failure in areas which cannot be quantified. The British Government has begun to face
up to this failure, but only because events have forced its hand.
Even then, it has tried to repair the injustices rather than examine the system which has produced these injustices. The consequence of the Callaghan visits may be a more just society,
if the reforms are honestly implemented, but it will not necessarily be a more stable society.

Northern Ireland sorely needs a new initiative, one generated
from within its own people. British intervention has been
necessary, to restore peace and to institute a move towards a
just society, but imposed policies can only go part of the way
towards solving Northern Ireland's problems. It is doubtful if
a final solution can be found within the present political framework—that is, the framework of party politics as now practised
in Northern Ireland, and the framework of present relations
between Northern Ireland, Great Britain and the Republic.
One advance would be to hold tripartite talks in which the
governments in Belfast, Dublin and London could define the
points on which they agreed or disagreed. It is apparent that,
in practice, all three governments accept that Ireland will not
be united without the consent of a majority of people in Northern Ireland, whether expressed through Stormont or through a
referendum. It might be possible to agree on a formula governing the North's constitutional position, and possibly on an
amendment of the Ireland Act to give the choice to people
rather than Parliament. But, within Northern Ireland, there
is need for stronger political expression of the will for change.
The initiative will never come from the present Unionist Party,
which still keeps the Orange card up its sleeve.